CW01239697

# The Yell-Free Parents' Guide to Disciplining an Explosive Child

*Positive Parenting Strategies to Stop Yelling and Become a Peaceful Parent*

Rachel Barker

© Copyright 2022 - Rachel Barker - All rights reserved

The content within this book may not be reproduced, duplicated, or transmitted without direct written permission from the author or the publisher.

Under no circumstances will any blame or legal responsibility be held against the publisher, or author, for any damages, reparation, or monetary loss due to the information contained within this book, either directly or indirectly.

Legal Notice

This book is copyright protected. This book is only for personal use. You cannot amend, distribute, sell, use, quote, or paraphrase any part, or the content within this book, without the consent of the author-publisher.

Disclaimer Notice

Please note that the information contained within this document is for educational and entertainment purposes only. All effort has been executed to present accurate, up-to-date, and reliable, complete information. No warranties of any kind are declared or implied. Readers acknowledge that the author is not engaging in the rendering of legal, financial, medical, or professional advice.

# Table of Contents

Introduction ........................................................................................... 5

Chapter 1: The Explosive Child ........................................................... 10

Chapter 2: Can an Explosive Child be Helped? ................................. 13

Chapter 3: The Explosive Child is Not a Brat but a Child That Needs Help .. 19

Chapter 4: Possible Casualties of Parenting an Explosive Child ........ 33

Chapter 5: Digging the Roots .............................................................. 37

Chapter 6: The Psychology of an "Uncontrollable" Child ................. 44

Chapter 7: Understanding the Explosive Child .................................. 53

Chapter 8: Dealing with an Explosive Child ....................................... 57

Chapter 9: Choosing Schools for Explosive Child .............................. 61

Chapter 10 The Parenting Art .............................................................. 66

Chapter 11: Managing an Explosive Child Away from Home .......... 70

Chapter 12: Improving Social Skills of Explosive Children ............... 76

Chapter 13: Understand the Factor that Contribute to Challenging Episodes ........................................................................................... 88

Chapter 14: Basic Principles for Dealing with an Explosive and Angry Child 94

Chapter 15: Strategies to Positive Parenting and Managing an Explosive Child ........................................................................................... 100

Chapter 16: Show Respect to Get the Respect of an Explosive Child .......... 103

Chapter 17: Teach Them to Accept Constructive Criticism ............. 106

Chapter 18: Your Marital Life Affects Your Child ............................ 111

Chapter 19: Help Children Express Themselves ............................... 116

Chapter 20: Strategies to Disciplining Explosive Children ............... 123

Chapter 21: Behavioral Therapy for Explosive Children .................. 127

Chapter 22: Multi-Modal Treatment ................................................. 134

Chapter 23: Techniques for Maintain Spiritual and Mental Well-Being ..... 139

Chapter 24: Empowering Your Child: Tools for Dealing with Uncontrollable Stressors ................................................................................................ 143

Chapter 25: Calming an Explosive Child ...................................................... 150

Chapter 26: Autism Spectrum Disorder - A Checklist of ASD Red Flags .... 153

Chapter 27: ADHD Symptoms and the Nature of the Disorder ................... 162

Chapter 28: What is the Distinctive Between ADD, ODD, and ADHD? ....... 172

Chapter 29: Prioritizing a Healthy Diet: What to Eat and What to Avoid ... 178

Chapter 30: Options for Handling Problems: Three Plans ......................... 183

Chapter 31: Other Practical Recommendations for Assisting Your Child in Coping with the Demands of Daily Life ...................................................... 190

Chapter 32: Physical Health Maintenance Techniques .............................. 196

Chapter 33: Emotional Development in Childhood ................................... 203

Chapter 34: Discipline vs. Consequence vs. Punishment .......................... 206

Chapter 35: Parenting Principles ................................................................ 213

Chapter 36: Time Management Tips .......................................................... 219

Chapter 37: Life Skills Your Child Needs to Master ................................... 224

Chapter 38: Build Your Child's Self-Esteem ............................................... 227

Chapter 39: Help Children Manage Anxiety During the Pandemic ........... 239

Chapter 40: Support Your Child During the Pandemic .............................. 245

Conclusion ................................................................................................... 247

*Author's Note* ............................................................................................. 248

# Introduction

These little folks are fantastic creatures here on earth. No doubt they can get wild sometimes, but that doesn't mean they are unlovable and, more importantly, hard to comprehend. Judging by the fact that you're hovering over books like Explosive Children, it can be understood that you are dealing with one, unfortunately.

It's not easy being a parent of an eruptive child, and it can be time consuming to figure out what's causing their rage. These children have difficulty adapting, have a poor tolerance for frustration, and have difficulty addressing problems. They frequently use anger to express themselves since they are having difficulty in these areas.

However, these outbursts of rage can cause issues at home and school. Fear not, parents looking for solutions to deal with their child's explosive behavior. There are options for dealing with it and reducing stress for both of you.

I established the Collaborative and Proactive Solutions (CPS) model based on my study with explosive children, which offers adults working with them a new method to approach things like discipline to solve their problems faster. The CPS model is based on the premise that "challenging behavior emerges when a child's capacity to respond adaptively exceeds the demands and expectations placed on the child."

It's not that these children are bad or manipulative; it's just that their brains can't handle the demands placed on them.

They lash out when their brains can't describe their problems or disappointments appropriately. Thus, it's all a matter of how you approach their actions. The CPS method, implemented in homes and schools across the country, is based on empathy for the child and developing a collaborative way for the adult and the child to deal with frustrations that works best for both. The CPS approach requires that the parent remain calm. Although it's easier said than done, it's critical. A child who is already frustrated will become even more so when someone is screaming at them.

Avoiding triggers is also beneficial, although it's not always possible. For example, taking a bath and going to bed are two of my four-year-old son's most dramatic tantrums. Obviously, we can't avoid these things unless I want to be up all night and have a stinky child. I utilize the countdown approach, telling him, "In 20 minutes, we will put on our jammies and get ready for bed." Before you take a bath, you can watch one more episode of your show."

It doesn't always prevent the tantrum from occurring, but my son can't claim he wasn't warned. I mean it when I say 20 minutes or one more episode. You can't let then talk you out of it because you don't want to get into a fight. You must be adamant about the actions you will and will not tolerate.

It's also crucial to get rambunctious children to use their words. The irritation that leads to lashing out is frequently caused by the child's inability to explain his or her thoughts or feelings effectively. In my house, we often say, "Use your words." My son has trouble expressing himself, especially when overwhelmed or frustrated. I remind him to utilize his words to get his point across if I catch him before he completely loses control. If he does not, I inform him that I am unable and unwilling to assist him until he does.

I applaud him when he calms down and utilizes his words. Instead of reinforcing the negative, praising children for their positive conduct can make an enormous difference. Having said that, how you respond to unpleasant behavior is equally critical.

Even if you use empathy, you must still deliver consequences. Though they don't work for everyone, some psychologists prescribe time-outs for children under the age of seven, which involve placing the child in a room with no toys or distractions until they calm down.

Finally, when they aren't upset or frustrated, strive to improve their behavior. Speaking with them about how to deal with huge or painful emotions, it's far easier to reason with them when they are not having a five-alarm breakdown than trying to reason with them while they're having an outburst. More effective coping techniques can be discussed. Breathing practices, for example, have been beneficial for my son. If he becomes frustrated, he will (on occasion) take a step back and take a few deep breaths to refocus. When he becomes irritated and I see a temper brewing, I tell him to "cool your thoughts," which offers him an alternate focus. If he can turn off some of those thoughts, he will be able to see things more clearly, and we will be able to avoid a catastrophic breakdown.

Giving explosive children the means to channel their anger is critical. Reaching out for professional help if you're unclear about how to begin to manage your child's explosive behaviors isn't a sign of failure. Their outbursts could have a deeper meaning, such as a medical diagnosis that requires treatment. However, without an expert opinion and diagnosis, you'll be doing a disservice to yourself and your child.

Empathy is essential, as is learning how to deal with them in a way that does not make people feel ashamed of their sentiments. The first step in building a more positive atmosphere for these children is to understand their triggers and strive to create healthy boundaries around them. They will eventually blossom if given the room to have their grievances recognized and valued.

Imagine a toddler throwing tantrums all the time, regardless of the location. Sound familiar? Now picture this: I had a long day at work, and when I reached the doorknob of my house's main gate, I saw the light of my lounge blinking abruptly. Startled by the way it looked from the outside, I stepped into my house anxiously to see my better half sitting on the chair right next to the kitchen with his hand covering his temples. He looked too frustrated, and to be honest, I had never seen him like this before. I asked what the matter was, to which he replied that our four-year-old had been having one of his tantrums and reached his extreme today.

In a rage of anger, he threw his little Hot Wheels car directly at the light bulb that sparked and shattered instantly. Our concern was not the light bulb that day but the rage and the extreme emotions that my little one expressed. It was a light bulb today, but what could it be tomorrow? To what heights would Simon go and damage things around him in his fits of rage?

We came upon the mutual understanding that we won't let our little Simon go any farther from this phase of his anger. We decided to deal with this problem as our topmost priority and see where we went wrong to make Simon intensely emotional. To our surprise, we found out that it was not our fault or something wrong with how we were parenting; instead, it was his cognitive development, and he lacked a few critical skills. Since then, we have been able to find the underlying cause of this condition and deal with our baby more attentively. That ultimately helped us deal with our explosive child more effectively, and we never faced any severe tantrums such as the "light bulb incident" ever again.

Do you want to know how? Of course, you do. However, before that, I would like you to know that you are not alone in this. Yours is not the first child who is hard to handle. Many children like yours who are left behind due to their cognitive underdevelopment. Unfortunately, parents don't always realize that there is more going on than a tantrum and treat it however they can, rather than productively helping their child learn how to manage the symptoms.

Why Should You Read This Book?

Dealing with explosive children is exhausting and, sometimes, frustrating. You feel as though giving up motherhood or fatherhood for that reason alone is a better option. It is perfectly okay to be overwhelmed by those feelings, but there is a way to improve the situation.

Explosive children require delicate attention and a few vital concepts which will help their behavioral development. This book details those concepts which will serve as a key to dealing with your "mini-hulk." From phases of parenting to the three Ds of dealing with explosive children, you will learn so much.

Rest assured, there is no rocket science involved. These are just some basic steps and knowledge that were researched thoroughly to help you understand your child better than ever, ultimately bridging the gap between your child's behavioral development and cognitive skills development.

So, grab a nice cup of coffee while your little monster is fast asleep or out and dive in. With time, you will learn methods that will change your lives and the way you parent forever.

"How do I tell if my child is explosive?" is a question parents often ask. There are no blood tests to confirm a diagnosis. Children who are "explosive" are simply those who grow angry more readily and often than others, and who express their irritation more severely with crying, shouting, hitting, punching, scratching, and damaging property than non-explosive children.

Honestly, I've never liked the phrase. In the first place, the term "explosive" indicates that these children's outbursts are abrupt and unexpected, which is not always the case—and this could be difficult to accept at first—but is generally accurate. Secondly, whereas many behaviorally demanding children erupt when they're furious (screaming and cursing as well as punching, kicking, biting, and spitting), many others collapse instead (crying, having panic attacks, and being cranky, withdrawn, and irritable).

In other words, even though the book's title refers to youngsters who are volatile, collapsing, or a mix of both, the tactics presented herein are appropriate for use with all children.

# Chapter 1:
# The Explosive Child

According to recent research, understanding the difference between a typical, antsy four-year-old and a hyperactive child to the extent that it affects their ability to learn is tricky as attention deficit disorders are becoming more prevalent.

A problem that manifests itself in persistent difficulty paying attention is recognized, especially when a child is entering the world of school. Obviously, in this context, the difficulties related to the problem of concentration are often highlighted in an almost dramatic way. It is in the classroom that it becomes evident how keeping up with the demands of adults, internalizing general social and behavioral rules, carrying out assignments, respecting allotted time, listening to the teacher, and staying still in one's seat can become a problem. However, at this stage, it is imperative to look for clues that may allow you to recognize any difficulties your child or other students may be having so that you can intervene at an early enough age. A young child may have behaviors that worry parents, such as opposing requests, being excessively energetic, and throwing too many tantrums. Still, some change and evolve with age. In contrast, others will remain unchanged or almost unchanged.

With this information, we can help when our child or partner is having trouble coping with rage. We also need to be aware that parental rage might be harmful to young children because it motivates us to exercise self-control.

Some parents spanked their children because that's how they were raised. Simply because hitting has been practiced for generations does not make it an effective teaching technique. It causes physical, neurological, and mental wounds, and it must end. We want to develop a loving link with our children, not break it. However, the moment a parent raises a hand in anger, even if it's to "teach a lesson," we're destroying the exact bond we're trying to form. Children's most important lesson from physical punishment is that they can't trust or rely on their parents.

Those who were hit as children can still help stop this toxic legacy. Parents must first practice self-discipline before disciplining their children. Put some distance between what provokes you and how you respond. Doing so will ensure you don't lash out in anger with violence.

Some argue that hitting is acceptable if it leaves no trace, yet it does leave evidence that have lasted centuries. We can break the cycle.

As a parent, you're aware that emotions can get the best of you. Children have an uncanny ability to push buttons you didn't even realize you had, and before you know it, you're screaming at the top of your lungs. You're not alone in this, and your parental dissatisfaction is understandable. The good news is that you can adjust how you communicate with your children, shifting from a furious monologue toward respectful discourse.

The secret of good parents is that they know how to raise good children. They uniquely communicate with their children and converse uniquely with themselves. They're approaching the whole parenting process from a different angle.

The difficult aspect of parenting, as any parent knows, is regulating our anger triggers. Regardless of your child's specific issues, you must work on yourself if you want to be a good parent. A child does not cause the anger or anxiety that draws us into power battles; our fear and mistrust cause it. Our early childhood traumas, big and small, are a part of who we are. They're also the part of us that takes control anytime we're disturbed; you must understand that when you're angry or scared, it's often an experience from your childhood driving your reactions.

We want our children to be successful in life, not in the sense of gaining the rewards that our society offers, but in discovering, polishing, and sharing their unique skills throughout their lives. We know how to assist children in doing so. Much of it has to do with managing our anger and allowing our children to explore and develop confidence and resilience.

Some children are born with temperaments that are more challenging to manage, and our inner work as parents is much more crucial for these children. No matter what your child brings, the way you respond to them when they come into the world will impact their ability to make the most of their life. Your child will amuse and frustrate you and thrill and annoy you equally. Your child will ask you to grow as well, almost by mistake. You can raise happy, emotionally healthy children who are successful in every way. However, you must learn to recognize when you're provoked and restore equilibrium before acting. You can ease your anxieties by reflecting on your own experiences and making peace with it.

# Chapter 2:
# Can an Explosive Child be Helped?

Explosive, volatile children are challenging to manage, and there are several things that a family can do to help their child. Counseling is usually the first step. A counselor may help ease the stress and tension in the family and help with problems affecting their child. The family should also talk to their child to help them understand how they are feeling, as children are generally unable to express themselves verbally or emotionally. Parents will also want to learn how to manage their emotions to prevent any negative consequences from their anger or frustration.

Parents should also be aware that they may not be able to change their child's behavior, as explosive behaviors and anger are usually learned over time. Children learn how to deal with anger by observing the behaviors of others, and parents need to be mindful of the examples they set for their children. Parents can also try to remove themselves from situations that could prove to be a trigger for their child's explosive episode, as this will limit their potential to act out.

In addition, parents should find non-aggressive techniques to solve problems that might arise between them and their children. They should also find other children with similar problems living in their community or the same social circle. The purpose is to help the child learn how to express themselves, and channel their aggression more productively. By bringing other children together, they can learn to relate to one another and healthily express themselves.

Parents will also want to limit their child's exposure to violent entertainment, such as movies and video games, and limit their overall time in front of television and computers. Children can learn how to use these outlets in place of a human being to express themselves, which can cause some issues once they are older. Parents need to be aware that explosive children may become aggressive adults if they do not learn to constructively manage their anger and aggression.

When parents manage their negative feelings and anger, their children will eventually learn these skills. For this to happen, however, a parent must be able to express his or her own emotions constructively.

Children understand what their parents feel because they have observed them since birth, which this can cause them to act out even when they don't want to.

Parents can also help their children by setting aside time for them to spend with friends of their choice. They will learn to be more confident and independent, which will allow them to age and act healthily. Parents should also designate a room in the home where they can go when they need to be alone, such as their bedroom or bathroom. As a result, a child will learn how to express themselves verbally and emotionally and cope with their anger and frustration appropriately.

Ultimately, parents must try to address their issues before trying to help their children. Children learn how to express themselves by observing how others behave around them, and parents and other children will have the most positive impact on their behavior. Parents should be aware that explosive children are often trying to communicate something through their actions. They will eventually learn to do so more effectively once they calm down.

They will be much more effective if they can keep their negative feelings and anger in check, as this can cause a child to act out in an even more aggressively. In general, these children are not bad children. They are usually just misunderstood and need someone who can help them deal with their rage in a healthy manner.

## Positive Parenting Strategies

Parents want to do the best for their children. Your child's behavior reflects how you parented him or her, but there are ways to change how you interact with your child.

Positive parenting is learning how to control yourself and what you say, understanding how your children feel, and teaching them how to deal with their feelings positively. Children are very emotional beings who act out in emotionally charged situations, but this doesn't mean you need to respond negatively.

Think about what your child does and how you feel when he or she does these things. Your child probably acts out because he or she is feeling something, whether negative or positive. You can tell your child what you think about their behavior, but you should also teach them how they can best express themselves when they are upset or angry.

Once you know how your child expresses themself, you can begin to set limits on their behavior to help them learn what's appropriate. It may also mean that you're going to need to set boundaries that will help your child feel safe and secure enough to express him or herself.

1. Do not engage in name-calling or verbal abuse.

Your child might have a quick temper and lash out at you for something you said. Regardless of how you feel, it's important not to yell or call your child names, as this is not safe for anyone involved. It's also important to know that name-calling and verbal abuse can make your child feel more upset and angrier. If you need to limit your child's behavior, take some time aside from the situation. Tell your child that you're setting a limit, and they can't just act out in anger.

For instance, perhaps during a lunch visit, your child is obnoxiously loud in the school cafeteria. It might be tempting to tell them to stop talking or take the food from them. However, that child will be more upset because they were only trying to communicate, and you took their food from them.

Instead, tell your child that you will speak to the teacher about the incident and will speak with them as soon as you're finished. Stepping away may allow your child to calm down a bit, which will enable him or her to be more receptive to what you have to say.

2. Do not shout or raise your voice when punishing your child.

Sometimes, parents must punish their children for them to learn how they should act in certain situations. Usually, this involves making the child stay in their room until they can calm down. However, if you're shouting at your child or raising your voice with him or her, this will not help them feel better.

Instead, try to speak calmly and rationally with your child. They will be more likely to listen to what you have to say that way, and you should feel confident that they will understand what they did wrong and how they can fix it in the future.

3. Keep in mind that you are your child's role model.

Children are very observant and will take cues from their parents' actions. When you want your child to stop shouting, you must control your own behavior. It would be best if you shouldn't yell during an argument or when you're upset about something else in your life.

Instead, it's critical to model how you want your child to behave in the future. It's vital that children feel that their parents love and care about them, regardless of limits on tolerance for their behavior. You can do this by making sure that you're sending them positive messages and supporting them in other ways.

    4. Keep calm when dealing with your child.

Always try to keep a level head when dealing with your child's behavior problems. It would be best for you to stay calm and rational, so your child will be more likely to listen to what you have to say. It is not the time to get angry with your child or punish them in a way that they might not understand yet.

It can be frustrating when you feel your child's behavior is out of control, but you must remember that you should remain in control of yourself as the adult in the situation. Consider practicing breathing exercises when you're feeling angry or stressed out. You might also consider counseling or asking a friend or family member to talk with you about your problems.

    5. Do not punish in a way that you will regret in the future.

Punishing your child is not the solution to behavior problems. If you're angry about your child's behavior and believe that they should be punished, keep in mind that this will only make them more upset with you.

Instead, remove yourself from the situation so they can't see how upset you are. Tell your child that you're going to do something else and that you'll talk to them when you're ready. They can calm down and may even end up being a positive experience for both of you.

    6. Respect your child's privacy and personal space.

Children are inquisitive and will frequently ask questions about some of their most personal feelings, such as what they do in their bedrooms at night or why their behavior isn't the same with their friends as it is with their family members.

While you should answer your child's questions, it is essential to respect their right to privacy when they ask these questions. If you feel that this is being regularly, then you might want to seek advice from a counselor about how best to handle the situation.

7. Do not use physical force to get your point across.

Although you might have had some experience in how physical punishments affected you when you were younger, it isn't something you should use on your child now. When you use physical force, it might seem like you're punishing your child for a moment.

However, physical punishment will only upset them more. It's also important to know that your child has the right to defend himself if they are being physically abused.

8. Convey to your child that you are in charge.

Although you don't want to physically punish your child for something they done, it's critical for them to respect your authority as a parent. They must feel as though they can always come to you in times of need, which means that they shouldn't be able to ignore you or your requests.

It's also necessary to let them know that you care about them and will do anything within your power to keep them safe and happy. It's best if they know they can trust you, which will make for a much stronger bonding between the two of you in the future.

9. Talk to your child about his or her feelings.

You need to help your child learn how to express emotions in a healthy way. However, it doesn't mean that you must regularly accept destructive or negative behavior from them. Instead, it means that you should work with them on their behavior and help them to understand the consequences of their actions.

If you find that they are being verbally or physically abusive toward other people in the home, you might want to change their environment. This could mean taking away a privilege they enjoy or putting them in time-out.

10. Teach your child how to solve problems in the future.

Children will run into problems with their friends and classmates throughout their lives. It's important for you to actively teach them how to solve problems in a healthy way. It means that you should encourage them to talk with their friends if they are having a disagreement or to ask for adult help if they feel as though it is necessary.

You can also tell them about problems in your home and explain how the problems were successfully resolved. In doing so, you teach them you have learned how to manage frustrations and anger, just as they are.

# Chapter 3:
# The Explosive Child is Not a Brat but a Child That Needs Help

Imagine the child you see in the supermarket, the one who makes you want to fall on your knees and exclaim aloud, "Thank God he isn't mine!" We're talking about the kicker, the spitter, the fit thrower, the screamer, the child who attacks parent and peer with such ease that you can't help but wonder if he's possessed. The issue arises when you are unable to simply walk away, shaking your head and wondering what went wrong with his parents, since you are the parent, he is your child, and he is coming home with you—as soon as you can drag him out to the car and find a way to keep him fastened in. What should a parent do?

"Why Is My Child Behaving This Way?"

When parents call to schedule a consultation for their child who is about to be expelled from kindergarten or who has pushed them to the brink of social isolation from neighbors and friends due to behavior problems, they have one question on their minds: "Why does my child act this way?"

This question must be answered for you to comprehend how to assist your child. As you will quickly discover, the explanation for why children explode is significantly more intriguing and intricate than the "brat" hypothesis.

The first step to understanding is to gain an awareness of the many types of explosions displayed by children. While many dramatic tantrums may appear and sound the same to the exhausted parent standing by, not all explosions are created equal. I will shortly demonstrate this to you. Before I proceed, I want to urge you to avoid falling into one of two traps. The first is the tendency to conflate symptoms with causes. When working with children who explode, it's natural to believe that the explosions are the source of the problem, or in medical terminology, the condition. However, common sense should tell you that children do not sit peacefully playing and then suddenly explode. Something concealed, something at work beneath the surface, sets them off repeatedly.

The second temptation is to group all possible causes of childhood explosions together and assert that there is a universal approach to treating them. This is equivalent to claiming that the same condition must cause a headache as a leg, stomach, or shoulder discomfort and that all of these can be treated with aspirin.

## As Icebergs Explode

Consider explosive outbursts to be like icebergs. The visible portion, the one-tenth that rises to the surface, is the yelling and screaming, the bulging eyes and flailing arms, the spitting, kicking, and swearing that exploding children unleash during their fits. The nine-tenths of the explosion that we cannot see is the cause. Here, we take on the role of detectives, delving into the enigma surrounding potent powerful forces.

Once you begin to evaluate all these forces, you will begin to understand why your child reacts in such a particular way to the world, and the blowups will make sense. In no way does this mean you will approve of or condone your child's explosive behavior. You will, however, gain a better understanding of what causes the eruptions to occur and will be better equipped to respond in a way that minimizes explosions.

The following two examples demonstrate the utility of the iceberg analogy.

Eugene and Manuel were both first graders who were committing peer assaults. Eugene fought at the bus stop. Manuel's assaults were primarily in the school cafeteria and occasionally in the school corridors and library. Prior to coming to my office, both children's parents attempted time-outs, loss of privileges, rewards, and talking/lecturing/yelling/spank-bargaining/bribing/counting without success. The assaults went unabated. Both boys faced placement in alternative educational environments. Their schools and other parents labeled the children as rebellious and explosive and demanded immediate action.

Eugene would strike most parents as quiet (mousy), apprehensive, and most emphatically not prone to the in-your-face, coequal-with-the-parent attitude that oppositional children and teenagers are prone to exhibit. At the bus stop, he would jump onto the backs of the other children and pull their hair, or he would use their coats or belts to pull them back off the bus's steps. He clawed a child's face so brutally on one occasion that she had to be rushed to the doctor.

On the other hand, Manuel was a stocky, tiny guy with a perpetual grimace. It was natural to believe he was capable of being an angry actor. His assault was more direct than Eugene's. He'd punch the child he was angry with directly in the face. Being roughly a third the size of many of his friends, he was capable of wreaking havoc. When I got to know Eugene more, I discovered an obsessive streak that characterized his thinking. He had developed the conviction that he needed to be the first on the bus every day. He would begin to anxiously whine as he walked to the bus stop with his mother if he noticed another youngster had arrived before him.

Every morning, Manuel's mother waged war with him that diametrically opposed what occurs in many houses. Most children must be threatened to leave on time to make the bus. Eugene would gladly have departed an hour early if his mother had tolerated it, and his need to arrive first produced tension at the breakfast table each morning. Eugene believed he needed to be the first on the bus in the same way that you and I think we need to breathe. The strength of this idea drove him to assault any child who attempted to pass him. Being first was a matter of life and death for him.

Now, let us return to our friend Manuel. He was diagnosed with a sensory processing disorder. He was not a worrier or a compulsive in any way. Rather, he possessed an acute sensitivity to touch and pressure. He detested tags in his shirts, and when he was younger, he was guaranteed to pitch a world-class fit if the toe seams of his socks were not perfectly aligned. He was often complaining about his clothes being too tight. He'd stretch his T-shirts' necks out so much that they practically slipped over his shoulder.

The result of this discomfort resulted in an excessive desire for personal bodily space, and even a minor touch against him threw him into orbit.

The bane of children like Manuel is that young children spend an inordinate amount of time at school standing in line. He felt assaulted when other youngsters bumped against him or rubbed against him. He retaliated in what he perceived to be self-defense. His perpetual frown was there because he believed he lived in a world where he was continuously under attack.

By recognizing the underlying causes of each boy's meltdowns, remedies were apparent, and I am pleased to say that Eugene and Manuel and their parents are now doing well. However, it was not without some early consternation over the underlying causes of their behavior.

## A Tantrum Taxonomy

Every child experiences tantrums, meltdowns, and explosions. It's a natural part of growing up. Often, these outbursts fall under the category of what I frequently refer to as typical. Which parent hasn't experienced the sensation of taking a child from a store, the child in tears and wrath about missing out on a particular toy? These incidents reveal little about a child's psychological operations, except that they are normal.

Tantrums, meltdowns, and explosions are legitimate concerns when your child takes them to an extreme not seen in other children. Your concern is justified when you learn that your child is a walking powder keg compared to his or her friends. If it becomes evident to you—through the comments of relatives, neighbors, or your child's instructors, or through the way other children shun your child—that anything is wrong, you must intervene.

I will ignore the embarrassing, yet natural fits and tantrums youngsters encounter because they fade with time and maturity. Instead, I will focus on the reasons and appropriate treatment of these tantrums and explosions that are certain to be detrimental to your child's happiness and achievement.

I believe that the primary cause of extreme explosive behavior in children (and, frankly, adults as well, which underscores the critical nature of early intervention for your child) is what I refer to as road-map meltdowns. Explosive children are prone to make presumptions about what will happen soon. These assumptions—their mental road maps of the future—can take the form of small "movies" depicting what they believe will happen next. In their imaginations, road maps are believed to be correct 100 percent of the time. They are guaranteed to happen.

When the child's anticipated event does not occur, his map disintegrates. Parents who claim their child acts as if their world has ended because they stopped at the drugstore instead of heading straight to the grocery store do not realize how accurate they are. When a child's road plan does not come to fruition, he is adrift for an instant. The spectacular tantrum that ensues demonstrates how overwhelmed some youngsters can become when confronted with something unexpected.

Additionally, there is the problem of defiant versus explosive behavior. I've noticed an alarming amount of confusion among parents, teachers, and others who engage with children over the terms "defiant child" and "explosive child," with many believing that these labels are interchangeable, that they are different ways of describing the same behavior. These are, in fact, two distinct sets of concerns. But while it is true that children who are "defiant" can be explosive, and children who are "explosive" can be defiant, the underlying personality characteristics of the two groups are entirely different and require treatment accordingly.

Defiant children (also known as "oppositional children") are not usually tense or apprehensive and are not particularly concerned by unexpected changes or happenings. Instead, defiant youngsters are acutely aware of the problem of power—who has it, how much they have, and how to demonstrate that no one can force them to do anything. At an astonishingly early age, they dislike being told what to do by anyone. They behave in such a way as to be on equal terms with their parents and other adults in terms of power and influence.

Another primary explanation of explosive behavior has nothing to do with psychology and everything to do with it. I will detail the role that allergies and food sensitivities can play in the development of explosive behavior in children, particularly in the age bracket covered in this book—three to ten years old. The fact that we rarely consider allergies and dietary sensitivities in the context of behavior demonstrates how blinded we have become. Parents and experts alike are prone to dive headfirst into elaborate behavior modification programs or long-term usage of mood-stabilizing drugs without considering the simple possibility that what youngsters eat, drink, or breathe may influence their behavior. We must rule out allergies and dietary sensitivities if the goal is to address the underlying reasons, not the symptoms.

Even among allergists, there is substantial disagreement on this subject. Simply put, over the years, a disproportionate number of the exploding, irritable children I have seen have bags under their eyes, flushed cheeks, a persistent runny nose, a history of ear infections, or background of bouncing off the walls after consuming certain foods or food additives. I am also all too aware of the youngsters I see diagnosed with serious conditions such as bipolar disorder, only to have their symptoms significantly improve following treatment for allergies or food sensitivities.

There are further critical considerations with explosive behavior that we should not overlook. For instance, generalized anxiety disorder and depression are two factors that contribute to explosive conduct. Children who are anxious or depressed are not smaller replicas of anxious or sad adults. They behave in a unique manner. Indeed, irritable, volatile conduct might be one of the primary indicators of these underlying anxiety and depression difficulties.

Additionally, there is the issue of childhood bipolar disorder. It is well-known that children who suffer from it can be highly unpredictable. There is, however, much controversy regarding the appropriate use of this diagnostic in young children. In part, the dispute centers on the absence of observed manic episodes in children, which some theorists feel is one of the essential signs for making such a diagnosis. Others say that tense, angry, and explosive conduct represents the beginning of childhood bipolar disorder, a precursor to future episodes. It's a tricky diagnosis to make because bipolar disorder appears to develop gradually. Its symptoms manifest gradually, until it becomes clear that bipolar illness is the accurate diagnosis. Bipolar children are almost always misdiagnosed along the way as suffering from depression or having attention deficit hyperactivity disorder (ADHD) or oppositional defiant disorder along the way. While no doctor has a crystal ball, I believe that many today attempt to diagnose bipolar disorder too early and treat it with medication before thoroughly examining other possible reasons.

What is the connection between attention deficit hyperactivity disorder and explosive behavior? While children with ADHD are frequently inventive and creative, they can be disruptive to an entire classroom, and their impulsivity and failure to predict the repercussions of their actions frequently result in explosions and altercations with adults.

Sleep problems and sleep-disordered breathing have been linked to explosive behavior in children, and these youngsters are commonly misdiagnosed as having psychological issues. Occasionally, simply removing either the tonsils or adenoids or both can make a world of difference in how a child behaves. Additionally, maturity plays a role in explosive behavior. It is a fallacy to suppose that a child's intellectual and emotional development go in lockstep. Yet how frequently have you heard an adult say of a child, "She is highly intelligent. Isn't she capable of acting better than that?" Children who are emotionally immature explode for reasons that have nothing to do with oppositional behavior and little to do with road maps. Their care must place a premium on social skills development in a way that other exploding children do not.

Children who experience an expressive language delay, a distinct developmental condition, are frequently frustrated by their inability to communicate with others. They often point and grunt during their formative years and can be explosive if they are unable to communicate their needs effectively. It is well established that children with language difficulties exhibit more troublesome conduct than children who do not have language impairments.

Children with learning disabilities and processing difficulties might become excessively irritated when they cannot grasp classroom skills that their peers appear to accomplish effortlessly. Frequently, when they refuse to participate in classroom activities, they are portrayed as explosive, rebellious, or belligerent. However, they are striving to protect their own dignity by not publicly exposing their academic inadequacies.

It is sometimes more important to consider what the world has done to an explosive child than it is to consider what the child has done to the world. Children's explosions might result from bullying, family instability, or poor parenting techniques. We should not be surprised by how a youngster behaves when he or she has lost his or her sense of security or when the frustrations of an unsafe world become intolerable.

## Why Should I Inquire?

There is overwhelming evidence that we are playing a high-stakes game. We must identify and treat the reasons for explosive behavior in children early in their lives to avoid lifelong issues. One study followed individuals from infancy to about age forty. The study discovered that the lives of ill-tempered boys were distinguished by poorer levels of professional performance and career satisfaction, lower military rank, and greater unemployment rates than their more even-tempered contemporaries. Ill-tempered girls are more likely to marry less successful men and become ill-tempered women and moms.

Given the variety of contributing factors to juvenile explosive behavior, we should never again think of a child's explosions in simplistic terms. I go deeply into the lives of youngsters in this book to discover the causes of their explosions to save them from a downward spiral. The good news is that once parents identify the factors affecting their child, the solutions are frequently quite simple.

Individuals usually inquire why I am so taken by explosive youngsters. When I reflect on my work, I realize that explosive children have always perplexed me the most. If working with children for nearly thirty years has taught me anything, it is that there will never be a clear answer for why children explode. The causes of these explosions, which are generally unknown, are incredibly diverse and span the medical and psychological spectrum. However, we live in a society that frequently dismisses the intricacy of these children's difficulties.

No child should be ostracized or rejected, even more so for the underlying causes of explosive behavior that we shall investigate. You will quickly discover that the factors underlying a child's explosive conduct are so powerful that your will be required to assist the child in regaining control. Additionally, you will quickly develop a more sympathetic picture of what any explosive youngster is experiencing.

No parent wishes to gauge the happiness of his or her family by the time since the last explosion. Neither does the child, regardless of her age, whether she is three, eight, ten, or even older. As is the case with many children, the explosive child is desperate for praise and acceptance. Children who experience huge blowups dislike the sensation they experience following the eruption. They get themselves into mischief at home and at school, and their classmates begin to avoid them. Ultimately, they begin to dislike their lives. There is no more compelling reason to begin your investigation into the underlying cause of your child's explosions than this.

# Bright Side of Being a Parent of an Explosive Child

Accepting Your Child's Behavioral Disorders

Dealing with an explosive child can be highly stressful and frustrating. Therefore, you must learn as much as possible about explosive disorders and do everything you can to help your child and yourself. You must devise strategies to assist you and your family in coping with and accepting the situation.

Creating Healthy Expectations

First, I want you to release the idea that there is not only one way to be happy and fulfilled. Secondly, let go of your current expectations and become more flexible in the image you have for your child. If possible, involve your child in this stimulating process. It gives them ownership and may encourage them to participate more fully. Make it fun, make it interesting, and gather as much input from them as possible. If your child is not able, involve their doctors or therapists in your vision to grasp what a realistic image looks like in the first place.

With genuine, realistic expectations, you can break down the ultimate dream into smaller achievable goals for you and your child. This is the big difference between realistic and unrealistic expectations. For example, if you are parenting with unrealistic expectations, you may open them to a life of ongoing frustration, stress, and sadness as your child cannot reasonably meet those expectations. However, when you parent with realistic expectations, you see finite progress toward those goals, and you begin to feel a sense of pride, accomplishment, and fulfillment with your child. The child will feel that positive energy which will lead to greater harmony between the two of you and a deeper bond that you can both share.

How to Cope Emotionally as a Parent

Let's be honest. It is upsetting to learn that your child has an explosive disorder. You might have guessed it. You may have thought that the symptoms and behavior your child has been exhibiting are symptoms of some disorder. Nonetheless, the doctor's official diagnosis is always overwhelming.

Overcoming emotional conflict and finding peace in acceptance:

- Allow yourself to be sad. As parents, we all have lofty expectations for our children: they will be well-behaved, high achievers in school, popular with their peers, and praised by teachers. When a child is diagnosed with an explosive disorder, this vision is shattered. It breaks your heart to realize that he will never behave like other children. Allow yourself time to grieve and avoid burying your emotions. It's OK to cry and be sad.
- Stop rejecting your child for who they are. Your initial thoughts will most likely be angry: "Why can't my child be like everyone else's?" Recognize but don't believe those thoughts. Instead, confront the beliefs.
- Consider the following. Do you love your child any less because they have a behavioral disorder? Do you hold them responsible for it? You probably love them even more and want to do everything you can to protect and shelter them. You adore your child regardless of who they are. It is another step in the right direction.
- Recognize your child's positive qualities and be thankful that they are healthy and robust. The explosive disorder does not preclude a child from being gifted and talented in a variety of areas. Because of their natural vitality and energy, those children are often highly gifted and creative. Concentrate on these assets and allow them to become a source of pride and joy for you.
- Don't feel bad about yourself. When parents learn that a child has a disease or disorder, their first reaction is usually guilt.
- Stop fighting reality. Refusing to accept the fact is a losing battle. When you find yourself against hope, your child will not suddenly change their behavior, nor will their symptoms disappear. You may even deny that they are sick at all, believing that it was a misdiagnosis, and rush to seek a second and third opinion.
- Ignoring the facts is emotionally damaging because an explosive child will never outgrow it and never behave like you expect them to. When you notice yourself having these thoughts, bring yourself back to reality. Your child requires your assistance and support, not your wishful thinking.

The goal of this is to shift your perspective to the process and accept your child's condition emotionally.

## How to implement more practical coping strategies.

- Take control of your stress. As a parent, the most difficult challenge you will face for an explosive child is stress. It is something you will have to deal with daily. Unless you have stress-reduction techniques in place, the consequences for your physical and mental health can be severe.
  Every day, set aside time for yourself to unwind and relax. Meditate, do yoga, exercise, and go for a quiet walk or soak in a warm bath. While your child is at school, engage in a hobby or go out for a quiet lunch with friends; whatever helps you relax should be done regularly to avoid burnout. It is not a luxury but rather necessary, especially if you juggle a demanding career with a challenging family life.
- Stress management will also help you be more tolerant and calmer when dealing with your child and less prone to rage or frustration. The more drama you can avoid, the better it will be for both you and your child.
- Participate in a support group. Encouragement and support from other parents in a similar situation are essential. Look for these groups online or on social media platforms—you'll be surprised at how many there are. It is a fantastic way to share your problems and concerns with other parents and exchange advice, tips, and experiences.
  If the group is close by, you can even plan to meet regularly and introduce your children to one another. Many support groups also host expert lectures to keep members up to date on the latest information on explosive disorders. They also organize family activities and outings.
- Change Starts with You (The Parent)
  Parenting your child correctly, regardless of whether your child is neurotypical or lives with a behavioral disorder, means you must create a parenting style that matches the needs of your child. Many first-time parents believe that they can choose their parenting style in advance and that their technique will automatically suit their child simply because that is the parenting style that feels best for them.
  Your child will come out with their personality, preferences, strengths, weaknesses, and needs. You, as the parent, must

create an adaptable parenting style that meets those needs so you can empower your child to grow up to be the best version of themselves. For parents of neurotypical children, the example of how they want their children to become seems clear-cut. For parents of children with behavioral disorders, your expectations may be different based on the level of ability that your child has.

Tips for Helping Your Family Cope

If you have other children, the first thing you should do is inform them that one of their siblings has a kind of behavioral disorder. Depending on their ages, simplify as needed.

Tell them that you expect them to assist their brother or sister whenever possible and to never, ever make fun of his or her condition. When this is done, never be afraid to impose strict discipline.

The entire family should implement the strategies listed below. Lead by example, and your other children will learn to behave and interact with their siblings in the same way.

Highlight the "benefits" of this disorder. Children with this disorder frequently have unique talents that can be nurtured and developed. Some examples include creativity, spontaneity, energy, and enthusiasm. Be deliberate in pointing out these gifts to your child regularly.

Assist your child whenever possible. For instance, when he is struggling with a particular task, encourage your family to assist with homework. Attend therapy sessions whenever possible.

Establish family and household rules and activities that will help your child succeed. Giving them shorter chores to complete, for example, or making a list of things they need to do so that they can cross each one off as they meet them. Structure and schedule playtime with siblings so that they can participate in the games they enjoy.

If possible, keep an eye on playtimes to ensure that the child does not become overly excited. Keep an eye out for fights between siblings or other children and intervene immediately. When assigning larger tasks, enlist the assistance of a sibling to assist your child in completing them.

Accepting Mistakes as an Opportunity to Learn

You, like every other parent, are bound to make mistakes. You have probably already made thousands by now, and there will be plenty more as you continue your journey of parenting. Even parents of adult children make mistakes and find themselves having to recover from those mistakes in one way or another, as mistakes are a natural part of raising children. As they say, children do not come with a manual.

Rather than punishing yourself for making mistakes or creating an unrealistic outlook of your abilities, you need to accept the fact that mistakes are inevitable. Sometimes, you will become overwhelmed and will have difficulty regulating your emotions. Other times, you might miss an important clue, and it could lead to your child having a meltdown which will disrupt the peaceful environment you strive to create. There are many ways that mistakes can be made, and many reasons why those mistakes may be made. Regardless of how they happen, though, you must understand that they are inevitable.

Learn to adapt to each situation, developing new strategies for how you will minimize the impact of your errors on future experiences. Shift your perspective to view mistakes as an opportunity to learn and grow as a parent. Every time you overreact, miss a cue, or have a negative experience with parenting, reflect on why that happened, and what contributed to your negative experience. See if you can identify the trigger, the moment where everything went wrong, and what could have been done to prevent that situation or reverse it once it started. When you use mistakes as motivation for learning, it becomes easier to forgive yourself and navigate any new challenges thrown at you in a more prepared, productive, and calm state if similar situations were to arise.

Take Care of Yourself

Ask for help from family members and close friends when you need some time off. You must have alone time to help you manage the stress.

Find ways to help reduce stress:

· Reading books

· Watching a movie

Your health is important; getting enough rest, eating the right food, and exercising keep you healthy and strong.

Best of all, cut yourself some slack and understand that you are not a magician, nobody's perfect, and know the value of a reliable support system.

Putting Your Safety Mask on First

You have had to protect your child mentally, emotionally, and physically from many involvements they have encountered that are not ordinary experiences for neurotypical children. Perhaps you have protected them by drastically adjusting their environment, dealing with bullies at daycare/school, or fending off adults who do not comprehend your child or your parenting experience at all. These occurrences can be exhausting and seemingly never-ending when you are protecting your child. They can also leave you forgetting to tend to yourself and your own emotions as you become absorbed with protecting your child from the world around them.

Increase Your Feelings of Gratitude

Upon confronting chronically challenging situations, it can be easy to develop negative mindsets toward those circumstances. When parenting your child, you may have negative emotions toward parenting, the day-to-day experiences you have with your child, or even your child themselves. Again, these are only feelings caused by troubling emotions, and they do not reflect the way you truly feel about your child. Still, if they linger long enough, it can make the entire experience of parenting far more frustrating and can damage your relationship with your child, as well as the way you behave toward and around your child.

Taking time to regularly express appreciation for your child's existence and for the opportunity as a parent is an important way to counter those negative feelings so that you can create a more realistic and positive parenting experience. Each day, express gratitude to yourself and your child.

# Chapter 4:
# Possible Casualties of Parenting an Explosive Child

Staying positive is always important and even more so when you are parenting a child with ADHD. However, that doesn't mean you shouldn't be prepared for the worst-case scenarios, too. Read on to learn more about the possible casualties of parenting an explosive child.

## Your Relationship with Your Child

Sometimes, parenting a child with ADHD requires a bit of toughness. And other times, it requires you to be as soft as a possible. All these shifts, as well as the rather rigid life you will organize around your child's life can have an impact on how they perceive you (now, as well as when they grow up into teenagers, and then into adults).

Be prepared for a relationship that might not always look bright.

## Your Relationship with Yourself

How you feel during the six months after your child is diagnosed with ADHD can affect how well you handle the frustration and stress of parenting a child with ADHD. The stronger your relationship was during the time leading up to diagnosis, the better your ability to overcome this adversity becomes.

There is no magic formula for building a strong relationship with your child before he is diagnosed; however, you can build a stronger connection as time goes on. And even more than that, you can build yourself into a stronger person (trust us, you WILL need this).

Do not blame yourself for what is happening. All the planning in the world cannot determine whether a child will develop ADHD, so there's no reason to feel guilty over this. Practice self-love and gratitude, instead -- they will be a lot more helpful.

## Your Relationship with Your Spouse or Partner

We get it: parenting with ADHD often doesn't make things easier at home. You may feel like you are battling against the entire world and that's okay! Family life is never easy when there is an ADHD child in it -- as we know all too well.

Make sure both you and your partner are on the same page in terms of parenting methods, behavioral cues, and techniques. Also, be sure you are both mentally strong to withstand what's coming towards you. Don't neglect your own relationship, either, because eventually, one of you will end up bitter and remorseful — that will not help anyone, not you, not your child.

## Your Relationships with Your Other Children

Having a child with ADHD can cause some dramatic changes in your other children's lives, not to mention their emotions.

For example, did you know that children with an ADHD sibling are significantly more likely to have emotional disorders as well? And that includes depression!

The good news is that your relationship with your other children will be strengthened if you treat them fairly. If you can do this, then there is a good chance they will learn from your lessons and rise above the challenges themselves.

## Your Friendships

It happens; out of necessity, you will be spending more time with your child than with your friends.

And while we are all for enjoying time spent with your child (it is definitely a good idea to make sure they occupy your time), don't neglect the people who love you and were there for you during the other times of the year!

Our relationships with other people are what keep us grounded, and you don't want to lose that or be left without a friend when you need them most. Take care of your friendships as much as you take care of your marital relationship and your relationship with your child. They might not seem as important in the grand scheme of things, but they are the "check-in" everyone needs — including parents of ADHD children!

## The Ideas You Once Had of "Normal"

Your definition of "normal" will severely alter over the coming years, and you need to acknowledge that. Accept it as it is and embrace the "new normal," there is no other solution. After a while, you will learn to not only accept this new kind of normality but genuinely appreciate it as well. Because what parent doesn't love the idea of a happy, energetic child?

## The Resemblance to the Parent You Thought You Would Be

Parenting with ADHD can take a toll on you. One of the ways you can change this is by altering your perception of yourself as a parent.

Here's what we mean: to be a good parent you must be willing to do anything for your child. Even if this means going against everything you believed in regarding parenting techniques and strategies (e.g., playdates, consistent rules, and consequences, etc.).

## Your Ability to See Yourself as a Capable Strong Parent

This is one of the most important parts of your journey. You must be able to see yourself as a strong and capable parent.

If you don't, then you will have a hard time making your relationship with your child work. The only thing that can get you through the next six months is seeing yourself as the best parent possible. However, if you want to go beyond this, start by admitting that this was not something that was planned for you, and that's okay.

Be prepared for everything, because this will allow you to create plans and take preemptive actions before things get completely out of control. You have a lot of bumps in your road, and nobody can deny that. The good news is that there is SO much information out there on how to be a good parent to an ADHD child! Sure, you will have to learn how to sift through the "fake news," but once you get a hang of that, you will discover the world is a supportive place for people like you, so you will always find solutions to your problems.

# Chapter 5:
# Digging the Roots

It may seem weird to say, but there has never been a good opportunity to be a parent or a professional who works with a child who has behavioral challenges. The reason for this is because a vast amount of study on neurologically demanding children has been gathered over the last 40–50 years, yet we all know quite a bit more about why they are problematic and how to treat them than we have at any previous time in history.

There is a wealth of fresh information that may help parents better understand their children's issues, and those new insights can help them react more compassionately, productively, and effectively. What a relief! To complicate matters, because you may have been using other lenses for quite some time, you will need to have an open mind while looking at the world through these new ones. While this book's techniques may be difficult to follow at first, they might also signify a shift in parenting style, which is something you may not have been used to.

As a result, you'll need to have an open mind as well as patience (both with yourself and with your child) as you experiment with different methods of engaging and solving difficulties. Parents of children with behavioral issues should read this book to feel more positive and confident in their ability to handle their children's troubles. If you happen to be the child's grandmother or grandfather, teacher, neighbor, coach or psychologist, this book should at the very least help you comprehend.

## Diagnosing Explosiveness – Why is He or She Like That?

Tantrums and meltdowns are particularly worrying when they arise quite often, quite severely, or beyond the age at which they have been naturally predicted, such as throughout the horrific twos and into preschool. As a toddler grows older, his or her hostility will become even more harmful to you and the other children around him or her. In addition, it might cause children significant difficulties at school and with their peers. If your child tends to act out, there may be an underlying issue that needs attention. Some of the probable causes of aggressive conduct are as follows:

ADHD (Attention Deficit/Hyperactivity Disorder)

Adolescent and adult attention-deficit/hyperactivity disorder (ADHD) is a persistent illness affecting millions of children and often persists into adults. Hyperactivity, impulsive conduct, and inability to maintain focus are all symptoms of attention deficit hyperactivity disorder (ADHD).

Additionally, children who suffer from ADHD may have low self-esteem, difficult interactions, and poor academic achievement. Symptoms might occasionally get less severe as you become older. Some individuals, on the other hand, never totally overcome their symptoms of ADHD. However, they may acquire skills that will help them be likely to succeed.

While therapy will not eliminate the symptoms of ADHD, it may significantly reduce their severity. Medications and psychological interventions are often used in conjunction with one another in treatment. Early detection and treatment might make a significant difference in the outcome of a cancer case.

Attentiveness problems and hyperactive-impulsive conduct are the most common symptoms of ADHD. Attention deficit hyperactivity disorder (ADHD) symptoms appear just before the age of 12, and even in some children, they are visible as early as three years of age. ADHD symptoms may stay with you into adulthood. They can be mild, moderate, or bad.

People with ADHD are more likely to be men than women. Boys and girls can have different behaviors because of this.

There are three forms of ADHD:

- The Predominantly Inattentive - most of the time, he is absent-minded. The bulk of symptoms is classified as inattentional disorders.

- Hyperactive and Impulsive - The major portion of the symptoms are characterized by hyperactivity and impulsivity.
- Combined - This is a combination of symptoms associated with inattention and symptoms associated with hyperactivity, impulsivity, and not paying attention.

A child that tends to lack attention can display various behaviors. When it comes to academics, failing to pay careful attention to specifics or making casual blunders are common. Have difficulty keeping concentrated on activities or games Appear to be uninterested in what is being said to them, especially when directly addressed. Have difficulties carrying through on directions and hence fail to complete academics or household duties. Work that requires concentrated brainpower, such as schoolwork, ought to be avoided or disliked. Items that are required for jobs or activities, such as toys, school assignments, pens, etc., are misplaced. Being prone to be easily diverted. Avoid doing routine tasks, such as household duties, by not remembering to perform them.

Typical Behavior vs. ADHD

The majority of normally developing children are distracted, restless, or impulsive at some point in their lives. Preschoolers are known for having difficulty focusing and being unable to maintain focus on a single task for an extended period. Even among older children and teens, the length of their attention span is often determined by their degree of interest.

The same may be said about excessive activity. Small children are typically enthusiastic, and they typically retain their enthusiasm long after they have burned out their parents' energy stores. Additionally, certain children simply have a greater level of activity than most others due to their genetic composition. The fact that a child is different from their peers or siblings should never be used to label them as having ADHD.

Problems at school are more likely to be caused by anything other than ADHD if a child has no issues at home or with peers. For youngsters who are restless or distracted at home, but whose academics and friends are undisturbed the same holds.

Sensory Processing Issues

A child's behavior might be difficult to understand because of sensory processing difficulties. Loud sounds or bright lights may cause them to get agitated or they may remark that their clothing is too tight. Clumsiness or difficulty with reflexes like buttoning may be an issue. Screaming or crying when their face becomes wet are two examples of excessive behavior in children.

When a child can't understand the data they get from their sensors, it results in these actions. Touching, listening, tasting, smelling, and sight are all representations of the five senses that make up the human body. Additionally, the child has two additional sensors that tell them where they are about the rest of the world.

The sensitivity of children with sensory difficulties may range from being normal to being extreme. Children with sensory sensitivities require more engagement. Crashing into objects is a favorite activity for them. Children that are sensitive to sensory input generally avoid it or become stressed by it.

A child's sensory issues might be exacerbated or triggered by a shift in their surroundings. When in a loud, busy grocery store, a youngster who is calm and rational in a quiet vehicle may become anxious and bewildered. They may throw a fit or attempt to flee.

Sensory processing disorder, or SPD, is a common diagnosis given by parents of children with sensory difficulties. Indeed, SPD isn't yet a recognized mental illness. Due to the high prevalence of sensory disorders among those on the autism spectrum, it is now accepted that sensory abnormalities are a sign of the disorder.

Due to a wide range of probable reasons for emotional outbursts and violence, a correct diagnosis is important to receive the necessary treatment. You might want to talk to your pediatrician first to see if they can help. They will be able to rule out any medical issues and then recommend you to a professional for further treatment if necessary. A qualified and competent child psychologist or psychiatrist can assist in determining whether there are any underlying problems present.

# What Kind of a Parent Are You?

Enough with the child diagnosis. Consider this: what kind of a parent are you? This is important because this child-parent relationship is not a one-way street. It goes both ways and it's important to look at it from both angles. Parenting styles have a significant impact on children. Therefore, determine what kind of parenting style you have opted for? Is it any good for your child? Is it any better for a child's growth? Let's dive in and find out how many kinds there are.

How you raise your child may have a direct impact on everything from her weight to her sense of self-worth. When it comes to raising a child, the way you relate to and punish them will have a long-term impact on how healthy their growth and development will be. There are four main sorts of parenting styles, according to the research:

- Permissive
- Uninvolved
- Authoritarian
- Authoritative

Permissive

Parents who are tolerant of their children's misbehavior are described as permissive. Most of the time, they only become involved when something major is going on.

They have a "children will just be children" mentality and are very flexible. They may not be able to hold up their end of the bargain when they do utilize consequences. In exchange for pleading or promising to behave, they may grant a child's wishes, such as returning privileges or letting him out of time-out sooner.

If you're a permissive parent, you're more like a friend than a parent. Parents often encourage their children to speak to them about their issues, but they seldom attempt to discourage their children from making poor decisions or engaging in undesirable conduct.

Uninvolved

It is common for parents who don't get involved to be unaware of their children's activities. There aren't many rules in the world. In certain cases, children may not get enough direction and care from their parents.

Those who aren't interested in their children's lives expect their offspring to take care of themselves. They don't

spend a lot of time or effort on satisfying the fundamental requirements of children. A lack of parental involvement might be a sign of neglect, although it's not necessarily deliberate. The physical and emotional needs of a child might be neglected if a parent has mental health or drug addiction disorders.

When parents don't become involved, it's because they are ignorant of their children's growth. And sometimes, they're just too busy with other issues, such as job, bills, and home management, to take care of themselves.

Authoritarian

Parents that enforce strict regulations on their children are known as authoritarians. When a child asks the reasoning for a regulation, authoritarian parents are known to answer, "Because I said so." Negotiation is out of the question for them, and their primary goal is to be obedient.

Children are also forbidden from participating in activities that require them to solve problems or overcome hurdles. There is no consideration for a child's feelings when they set the parameters and impose punishments. In certain cases, authoritarian parents may resort to using punishments to discipline their children. As a result, instead of teaching children how to make better decisions, they're more concerned with making them feel terrible for themselves for their actions.

Rule-following seems to be the norm for children raised by stern, authoritarian parents. There is a price to be paid for them to obey you.

Authoritative

Rules and punishments are used by authoritative parents, but the views of their children are also taken into consideration by these parents. In this way, parents show that they care about their children's emotions while simultaneously letting them know that they are in control.

Authoritative parents spend a lot of time and effort trying to prevent their children from developing behavioral issues in the first place. In addition to praise and rewards, they use positive disciplinary tactics to promote good conduct.

Those with authoritative parents are more likely to grow up to be responsible adults who can communicate their thoughts and ideas without fear of reprisal. Happier and more successful children are often the result of a well-instilled sense of authority. Making judgments and assessing safety threats on their own is also more likely to be their strong suit.

Don't worry if you have periods of being lenient and others when you are more authoritative as a parent. This is normal. When juggling work and family obligations, it may be difficult to maintain a steady routine. Don't succumb to parental guilt or humiliation. In the end, it's not going to help.

In the end, research shows that the greatest way to raise children is via strict, direct authority figures. Although you may relate better with other parenting styles, there are actions you may do to establish yourself as a more authoritative parent.

To maintain a good connection with your child, you need to be dedicated and committed to becoming the nicest person you can be. Eventually, your child will prosper from your firm leadership style.

# Chapter 6:
# The Psychology of an "Uncontrollable" Child

When you're solving any type of problem, it's important to understand the root cause. Imagine that you're working on fixing up a house, and the walls are cracking, so you need to patch them up. The patching might work fine for a few months or even a couple of years, but soon those cracks will start coming back. Why? Because the cracks are just a symptom of the true problem... the foundation is crumbling. To fix the problem, you must fix the foundation.

Human struggles are the same way. Emotional dysregulation, temper tantrums, non-cooperation, rebellion, negative communication... those are all symptoms of a bigger, more fundamental issue that is going on within a person. To truly connect and solve the problem and strengthen the relationship at the same time instead of damaging it, the underlying problem needs to be addressed.

Here, we will try to help you understand the root causes of behavior and emotional challenges that you might have already experienced while raising, teaching, or caring for children.

## Defining Disorders

Before we get into a discussion of possible "disorders" a child might have, it's important to define what a disorder is. Disorder literally means "out of order." It's a pattern of behavior that is outside the variation of normal child ups and downs. Raising children is difficult and raising them when they have patterns of disruptive behavior that are outside of the normal range of childhood tendencies is exhausting, frustrating, consuming, and can even be life-altering if you don't get the help and resources you need. You need to understand whether your child is going through a regular life stage or if it's something more serious. This usually isn't easy.

Let's take the good old "temper tantrum," for example. Temper, like a temperature, or to temper something down, means a level. A temper tantrum is a child's level of emotion getting high and out of control, often seemingly out of nowhere. (However, most emotional outbursts or struggles aren't ever "out of nowhere" to the child, even if it seems like it to us on the outside.) A temper tantrum is a normal occurrence during childhood; children are learning how to regulate their emotions, how to name and identify these feelings, and what causes them. They're learning how to react, respond, and cope with the big feelings that are seemingly too big for their little bodies to handle.

However, although temper tantrums can feel exhausting to deal with as a parent or caregiver, they don't necessarily imply that your little one has a problem with authority or struggles with an attention disorder. Labels and diagnoses are a dime a dozen these days: many professionals and doctors want to be able to put a label on a child so that they can prescribe them medication, and many parents want a diagnosis for their child so they can feel like they have an "answer" to what they're struggling with. But humans are complicated, and all the emotions and symptoms of struggles that we exhibit don't always boil down to one "problem." Labels and diagnoses should be kept at a minimum.

As an adult looking for a solution to your child's seemingly problematic behavior, you should first understand why children behave as they do. Challenging behaviors can stem from myriad roots: health conditions, unmet emotional needs, lack of or too much stimulation, or genetic traits that can cause struggles, among many other causes.

The term 'disorder' should be used cautiously for children under five years old, as this is a rapid developmental stage. Children who are struggling with emotional or behavioral dysregulation, tantrums, or communication problems will often level out as they grow. However, educating yourself on signs, symptoms, and possible solutions is a smart way to prepare yourself in case things continue to get harder and you need more resources.

Some common early childhood emotional and behavioral conditions that we will explore include Disruptive Mood Dysregulation Disorder (DMDD), Oppositional Defiant Disorder (ODD), conduct disorder, and Attention Deficit Hyperactivity Disorder (ADHD).

Disruptive Mood Dysregulation Disorder (DMDD)

Disruptive Mood Dysregulation Disorder is signified by extreme irritability, anger, and frequent, intense outbursts of emotion. Children struggling with this disorder are at a level beyond an ordinary "moody child." This disorder shows severe emotional impairment that warrants clinical attention.

Someone with DMDD might be irritable or angry for most of the day, almost every day. They often have trouble functioning in one or more of their usual places, such as home, school, or with peers, because of said irritability. Their temper outbursts are severe, causing stress or damage to material things or relationships. Young people struggling with this disorder tend to use services and hospitals at higher rates than normal, endure suspensions and expulsions from school, and are prone to developing other mood disorders, such as attention deficit/hyperactivity disorder or also generalized anxiety disorders.

The difference between the typical irritability and severe irritability is that the latter is characterized by the inability to tolerate frustration. Every child, every person , becomes irritable from time to time. We all get frustrated; irritation is a natural reaction to this. Outbursts are out of proportion compared to the problem at hand. Typical irritability comes and goes and can often be tempered quickly or with ease. Severe frustration that comes with DMDD can happen at the drop of a hat, without signs leading up to it, and for reasons that one might not see as a normal "trigger" for an outburst. They can't be solved or soothed without a great deal of attention, communication, or negotiation. These outbursts occur frequently, at least a few times a week.

Children with this disorder are usually diagnosed between six and 10 years old. They need to have been experiencing symptoms for at least a year to qualify for this disorder. These symptoms often evolve with age. For example, an adolescent struggling with DMDD might have fewer tantrums as they grow, but signs of depression and anxiety begin to take their place instead.

DMDD is relatively new, as far as mood disorders go. It has only been in the Diagnostic and Statistical Manual of Mental Disorders (DSM) since 2013. DMDD can be treated with a variety of medications or psychotherapy—often a combination of both, but since there hasn't been a great deal of research done on this disorder, current practices are based on other closely related disorders. "Talk therapy" is showing many benefits and is usually used before medications are prescribed.

If you feel that your child is experiencing symptoms that might warrant another look, then talk to their doctor and report what you've observed, as well as what you've learned through your own research and anecdotal evidence from others. Your child's healthcare provider can help clarify the situation, put things in perspective, and help you plan for next steps.

It's also a good idea to get a second opinion from a mental health professional. These types of doctors have experience working with youth who struggle with mental and/or emotional disorders that goes beyond a typical pediatrician's practice. They'll be able to help you determine whether your child is struggling from multiple disorders at once and if so, what the appropriate methods for treatment might be.

Oppositional Defiant Disorder (ODD)

Oppositional Defiant Disorder is a type of behavior disorder that is usually diagnosed in children. Young people with ODD are defiant, uncooperative, and hostile toward their parents, peers, teachers, and other authority figures. They often cause more trouble to others than they do to themselves. Symptoms include seemingly constant arguing with most adults in a child's life, frequent "temper tantrums," refusing to follow instructions, always questioning rules, speaking harshly to those in authority, and seeking revenge against those who try and enforce regulations.

Researchers don't know what causes ODD, but there are two main theories. The first is the developmental theory, which states that this disorder begins during the toddler stages of life, between 18 months and four years old. Researchers believe that children developing ODD at this stage struggled to learn independence from a caregiver or other person to whom they were emotionally attached. The learning theory states that negative signs and symptoms of ODD are learned behaviors that come from one's environment. Here, researchers believe that children exhibiting signs of ODD are reflecting negative reinforcement shown to them by authority figures in their lives. Continued use of negative reinforcement just exacerbates ODD behaviors because the child is receiving what they crave: reaction and attention.

This could be put up alongside the "nature vs. nurture" theories of personality—are our behaviors, personality, and traits ones that we come with genetically and cannot be avoided, or do we pick them up from our families and experiences? During toddler and teenage years, even children on the "normal" scale of emotions exhibit behaviors similar to ODD. Almost every child experiments with disobedience, arguing, or going against authority, especially if they aren't in a calm state or are hungry, tired, or otherwise upset. However, in children with ODD, these symptoms are the norm, not the exception.

Diagnosis of this disorder should be sought from a healthcare provider, as they will observe the child, compile situational reports from adults, and look for patterns of behavior with possible causes. Treatment includes family, cognitive-behavioral, and peer-group therapy, as well as medications. The earlier that diagnosis and treatment happens, the easier it will be to prevent this disorder from overtaking your child's life.

Parents can help their children by participating in and speaking about therapy in a positive light, following up on and being consistent with appointments, working in a partnership or team with the healthcare provider(s), and reaching out for support when needed.

Prevention isn't necessarily possible, as researchers don't yet understand what causes this disorder. However, it can be possible to take steps to make ODD unlikely. Children exhibiting tendencies toward aggression and uncooperativeness can benefit from early intervention programs that teach anger management and social skills. Talk therapy and school programs to teach about and prevent bullying can also help children in the middle childhood and teenage years. Programs aimed at parent management are also helpful as they give parents the skills to react appropriately to their child's difficult behavior instead of in a way that is inflammatory or that causes the child to shut down.

Conduct Disorder

Conduct disorder the name for a set of emotional and behavioral problems that usually begin during adolescence or childhood. Children with this disorder have a difficult time following rules and behaving in a socially acceptable manner. There are three types of this disorder, categorized according to the age at which the symptoms first present: childhood, adolescence, and unspecified onset.

It can be mild, moderate, or severe. Symptoms are classified into four categories: aggressive conduct, deceitful behavior, destructive behavior, and violation of rules. Boys are usually more likely to engage in aggressive and/or destructive behavior, while girls tend to engage in deceit and rule breaking.

- **Mild Conduct Disorder** – Often, a child exhibits enough of the below behaviors to warrant a diagnosis but not more than that. Problems only cause minor amounts of harm, such as lies, skipping school, or breaking curfew.
- **Moderate Conduct Disorder** – If a child exhibits numerous behavior problems that have a mild to severe impact on themselves or others, they will usually fall into this area. Theft, vandalism, or substance experimentation would fall into this category.
- **Severe Conduct Disorder** – If your child's behavior is above mild or moderate, and their choices cause considerable harm to themselves or others, including sexual assault, weapons use, or breaking into property, they would be classified as severe.
- **Aggressive conduct** – This includes intimidation tactics or bullying, harm to people or animals, forced sexual activity, and/or using or threatening use of weapons.
- **Deceitful behavior** – This includes lies, breaking and entering, theft, and/or forgery.
- **Destructive behavior** – This includes things such as arson, vandalism, slashing tires, or things of the like.
- **Violation of rules** – This includes things like truancy, running away, substance abuse, and young experimentation with sexual behavior.

There are theories for environmental and genetic causes of conduct disorder. Environmental factors include an abusive childhood, severe family dysfunction, prevalent substance abuse in the home, and extreme poverty. Some research links damage to the frontal lobe (the part of your brain responsible for problem-solving, memory, emotions, and personality) with conduct disorder, causing struggles with impulses, inability to plan and think about future consequences, and an inability to learn from past mistakes.

Children who live in an urban environment, grow up in poverty, who have a family history of mental illness or conduct disorder, and/or who were abused or have a history of chronic trauma are all at higher risk for conduct disorder. Males are also more likely to develop this than females. Diagnosis and treatments are best handled by a mental health professional with the parents' input and support as a united team wanting an improved situation for the child. Children must exhibit at least three behaviors in a continued pattern within the past six months. The behaviors must also impair their functioning at school or in social settings.

Since conduct disorder is so highly influenced by environment, children struggling with this disorder will often be placed into another home. If there is no abuse present in their main home, however, and the parents can provide for the child appropriately, then talk or behavioral therapy will be used to help the child learn to appropriately express their emotions and/or anger. The team of professionals working with the child should also work with the parents, teaching them how to respond to their child and manage their own behavior. Long-term treatment is the norm, but catching this disorder early helps to make the prognosis more positive.

Attention Deficit Hyperactivity Disorder (ADHD)

Attention Deficit Hyperactivity Disorder (ADHD) is often confused with or mislabeled "ADD," but Attention Deficit Disorder is a different diagnosis. ADHD most often starts in children and may continue into adulthood (usually presenting before the age of 12, sometimes as early as three years old).

This disorder is characterized by inattention (wandering off tasks, lack of persistence), hyperactivity (moving about constantly, even when it is inappropriate or unnecessary for the specific task at hand), and impulsivity (making hasty decisions in the moment without thinking about the potential harm). Children with ADHD are usually placed into one of three subtypes: mostly inattentive, mostly hyperactive or impulsive, or a combination.

Symptoms of inattention can fall within the following:

- Failing to pay attention to details or making careless mistakes
- Trouble staying focused, both in academics and in play
- Not listening, even when addressed directly
- Struggle to complete tasks, schoolwork, or chores
- Difficulty organizing required activities
- General dislike or avoidance of activities that require mental effort

- Frequent loss of materials, toys, or school items
- Ease of distraction
- Forgetfulness of routine daily activities

Symptoms of hyperactivity and/or impulsivity can fall within the following:

- Frequent fidgeting or squirming
- Trouble staying seated or still
- Being in "constant motion"
- Climbing, running, or moving around when inappropriate
- Struggling to play or engage in quiet activities
- Seemingly constant talking
- Interrupting
- Trouble waiting their turn
- Intruding on others' space, activities, or conversations

Remember, as with other disorders, it is normal for children to exhibit behaviors like these here and there or in certain types of situations (e.g., when overstimulated, tired, hungry, frustrated, or cooped up). However, once these become a consistent pattern and start to negatively affect the child's home, school, and social life, then it is probably time to seek professional help.

Risk factors for ADHD include genetics, low birth weight, brain injuries, exposure to environmental toxins, and maternal drug use while pregnant. ADHD is more common in males than in females and is more common if other family members have it as well. Diagnosis requires a comprehensive examination by a licensed clinician such as a psychiatrist, psychologist, or pediatrician. Treatment options include medication and psychotherapy.

An ADHD diagnosis doesn't directly cause other disorders. However, children who struggle with ADHD are more likely to also develop conduct disorder, ODD, general mood and/or anxiety disorders, substance abuse, learning disabilities, tics, disruptive mood dysregulation disorder, and/or to be placed on the autism spectrum.

# Tips for Parents When Dealing with a Disorder or Diagnoses

If you and your family are struggling with the symptoms that show potential for a mood disorder diagnosis or have been diagnosed and don't know where to turn next, there are many ways you can help get your bearings about you.

- **Do your own research** – There is so much information out there. Look for news articles about the disorders, search out videos from reputable sources, and read books that they recommend. Stay up on clinical trials. Talk to professionals and ask questions about risks, benefits, and treatments. You have options, so don't take anything at face value if it doesn't sit well with your gut.
- **Talk to the professionals who know your child** – There's nothing more valuable than the experiences of your child's own teachers, counselors, or school psychologists. Not only are they experienced in their field, but they can apply that knowledge to your child specifically. They can also help you come up with plans in the interim until long-term goals are decided upon.
- **Manage your own stress** – If you aren't in a calm, peaceful state of mind, you won't be able to help your child get there either. Having a child with a mood disorder is stressful, but you can implement self-care strategies to help make sure you're handling it all to the best of your ability.
- **Seek support and help for yourself, too** – Your child isn't the only one struggling. It's important for you to have support groups, your own counselor or therapist, and people who you can speak to about everything you're feeling and dealing with.
- **Enable open communication across all lines** – Every resource and support person you have, including health care providers, is part of an intricate team. Keep the professionals up to date with plans and goals and involve your child in the discussion and options for treatment. When everyone can work together more closely, it will help ensure success.

# Chapter 7:
# Understanding the Explosive Child

From a renowned clinician and pioneer in this profession, a breakthrough method to understanding and parenting children who frequently demonstrate extreme fits of temper and other intractable behaviors.

What constitutes an explosive child? A youngster who expresses excessive frustration when confronted with routine problems—crying, yelling, swearing, kicking, slapping, biting, spitting, and destroying property, among other behaviors. A child whose frequent, serious outbursts leave his or her parents irritated, fearful, frightened, and in desperate need of assistance. Many of these parents have used all available options—reasoning, explaining, disciplining, sticker charts, counselling, and medication—all to no avail. They are at a loss as to why their child behaves the way he or she does; they are perplexed as to why the tactics that work for other children do not work for their child; and they are at a loss as to what to do instead.

Dr. Ross Greene, a renowned clinician and pioneer in the treatment of children with social, emotional, and behavioral difficulties, has worked with thousands of explosive children and has some good news: these children are not attention-seeking, manipulative, or unmotivated, and their parents are not passive, permissive pushovers. Rather than that, explosive children lack critical skills in the domains of flexibility/adaptability, frustration tolerance, and problem solving, necessitating a shift in parenting style.

Dr. Greene gives a fresh conceptual framework for comprehending their issues throughout this compassionate, intelligent, and useful book, based on neuroscience research. He discusses why traditional parenting and treatment are frequently ineffective with these children and what to do in their place. Rather than focusing on rewards and punishments, Dr. Greene's Collaborative Problem-Solving model advocates for collaborating with explosive children to resolve the issues that contribute to explosive episodes and teaching these children the skills they lack.

## Parenting A Child Who Is Explosive

Parenting an explosive child is akin to living on a battlefield. The sole distinction is that no combat training is provided. There is no preparedness for an invasion. There is no heavy artillery to assist you.

When the time comes, you are completely alone. With one mission... ensure that everyone makes it out safely.

All the hours you've spent scouring the internet seeking tools to help you calm down and tactics for emotional regulation. All the sleepless evenings spent researching and learning about your explosive child's fight or flight response. All the money you've spent on endless hours of classes and therapy sessions... it's all gone when it matters most. When your son erupts, none of this is present.

One thing is certain. Every explosion results in casualties, whether or not they are visible to the naked eye. Indeed, I've discovered that no one discusses or wishes to acknowledge these casualties since they are rather terrible. After tonight's conflict, I want to educate the public about what it's like to parent an explosive child.

However, more than anything... I want you to know that you are not alone if you find yourself in battlegrounds, because it is one of the most frightening places a parent can find themselves.

## The Unexpected Costs of Parenting an Explosive Child

1: The Relationship You Have with Your Child

You recall the day you returned him from the hospital. He was very diminutive. So incredibly lovely. All he desired was you, and you desired just him. Years later, you find yourself sneaking into his room while he is sleeping to receive the same caress and snuggle. You understand with each conflict, you are gradually drifting further and further away from the small infant who once snuggled against your breast.

2: Your Self-Relationship

You used to exercise at the gym. If you're honest with yourself, you had a cute body. Now, you're hardly able to muster a shower. After extinguishing all fires, bandaging all wounds, and cleaning up the mess, you simply collapse onto the couch or bed and prepare to do it all over again the next day.

3: The Relationship Between You and Your Spouse or Partner

Even the most perfect marriage or love on Earth cannot sustain continuous shooting at the village gates. Without a certain, one of you will become exhausted and weary ahead of the other. One of you will be driven only by the need to safeguard the family. Date nights devolve into therapy sessions, and late-night embraces devolve into late-night sobbing.

4: The Relationships You Have with Your Other Children

When you envisaged your family, you never anticipated it would generate memories through crisis management. You never imagined that you would be forced to enter the bunkers or, worse, that you would be forced to send them into the bunkers alone so that you could fight the battle alone. You fantasies of the day when you can give each child your entire attention, but you recognize that this may never be possible.

5: Your Relationships

Suddenly, your friendships begin to fall into two kinds. Those who make an earnest attempt to understand and those who gradually slip away because you lack the time to check in and give them the attention they deserve. You cross your fingers in the hope that your next conversation will not begin with "How are things?" Because, while you despise lying, you know they don't want to hear the truth.

6: Your Former Concepts of "Normal"

I am aware. Everyone has their own "normal." However, this is not the case. You long for the day, the week, and the year, and you can almost foresee what your "normal" will be. You lament the family portrait you hoped to create and cry over the memories others are creating.

7: The Parent You Assumed You Would Be

You've perused the literature. You've conducted the necessary research. You were certain about the type of parent you desired to be. And this... this is nothing like what you envisioned.

8: Your Self-Concept as a Capable, Strong Parent

It begins to weigh on you as battle after battle, decision after decision occurs. Well-intentioned friends tell you that you are an incredible mom who is doing the best she can.

However, you do not feel like a good parent. You are not in a state of strength. You lack confidence.

At the end of the day, every single casualty is justified. After collapsing outside the bedroom door and leaning against it, you close your eyes and recall that first night.

His skin, his scent, his evident love for you from the moment you first laid eyes on him. That. That is what strengthens you and prepares you for the next battle. That is what propels you back into the fray. Your infant requires your presence.

Bear in mind that you are not alone in your struggle. You cannot fight without the support of an army. You may have never met your army and may be unaware that they exist, but I assure you... you are not alone!

I make no claim to having all the answers, but I do wish to serve as your army... However, I will fight beside you. Because I understand how overwhelming life can feel, I've prepared something special for you that I'm overjoyed to share.

# Chapter 8:
# Dealing with an Explosive Child

Children tend to have a lot of energy and that's perfect. It means they are healthy and happy and that they are doing what children do best: exploring the world and learning about it at their own pace (which, let's face it, can be a speedy one).

Dealing with an explosive child is an entirely different affair though. An ADHD child is not merely energetic, they can be rambunctious, and what's worse, they can end up hurting themselves.

## Don't Worry Too Much About a Diagnosis

You will meet many well-meaning people on your child's road to diagnosis. Many will be doctors but others may be teachers, psychologists, speech therapists, and many other professionals. These are the people who will be your allies in the fight for your child's treatment plan through their guidance and advice.

You could also meet some less well-meaning people including school administrators, social workers, and teachers. They may show little to no understanding of what ADHD means, and more than that, they may show little to no interest in ever learning about it.

What is important, however, is to hold your ground. A diagnosis is just that: a name on a page that theoretically helps medical professionals and therapists find better solutions. Beyond that, however, what is essential is to help your child get their behavior under control and show them how to manage themselves when their symptoms are flaring.

## Explosive Children May Lack Some Cognitive Skills

Keep in mind that explosive children are not just overly energetic. They might lack important cognitive skills that help them regulate their energy levels, attention, focus, and learning capabilities. That is precisely why it is SO important for you as a parent to teach these skills to your child and show them "the way."

For instance, self-awareness is an important skill children with ADHD should learn.

What is self-awareness? It's the key to having a positive relationship with yourself. If you don't know how you act in certain situations and what triggers those reactions, it's hard to react positively.

## Expectations Outstrip Skills

Explosive children tend to have lofty expectations of themselves. They tend to think they are capable of more than what they can deliver. As a result, explosive children regularly let themselves down as well as disappoint their parents.

The reason for this is that explosive children are often not as capable as they think and may act before thinking while lacking the cognitive skills necessary for their daily lives.

It is important to help your child manage their expectations when it comes to the skills they have and the skills on which they still must work. Of course, you want to show them as much positive reinforcement as possible, but only when the situation requires it. Do not lie to your child saying they're doing well with something they aren't but emphasize the things they are doing well on and the things they are slowly mastering.

## Figure out Your Child's Specific Situation

Not all ADHD children are the same. Some may be more focused in certain situations, some may be completely hyperactive in other situations. Figuring out which skills your child lacks and which expectations they are not managing properly is essential for their development precisely because it will help you, the parent, guide them in the right direction.

## Try a New Parenting Plan

Gone are the days when you could treat the symptoms of your child's ADHD and hope things get better. While a diagnosis may help you identify some of the underlying causes, it doesn't simply mean that you can wait for your child to learn on their own.

Once you get a diagnosis, it is essential to figure out a new parenting plan that will bring more structure into your child's daily life. And if that parenting plan doesn't show the expected results, you should be prepared to adopt a new parenting plan. Change and adjustments are frequently required, so mentally prepare yourself for some fine-tuning in how you parent your child.

## Solve Problems Proactively

Explosive children tend to be reactive when it comes to solving problems. They tend to react after they have already made a mess of things and then they explode.

What you need is a proactive solution—something that preemptively prevents the situation from reaching the explosion point and that teaches your child how to solve problems before they are faced with an explosive situation.

## Prioritize Problems Before Solving Them

There is a difference between explosive children and other children when it comes to problem-solving. Explosive children will tend to attempt solving problems in a very freeform manner.

They will usually tackle all kinds of different problems if they are excited about doing so while neglecting other problems that could be more important or more urgent.

You need to prioritize the problems your child has and work on fixing them one at a time without allowing your child to distract themselves with smaller, less important issues or tasks.

The same applies to how you tackle your child's skills as well. Is it more important for them to make eye contact with other children or to keep them focused for more than three minutes at a time? Focus on the things that affect your child more directly and which could have a long-lasting effect and tackle those first. Then, move on to other skills.

## Don't Mislabel Your Child

Remember that your child suffers from a disorder that affects them in many ways. They are not just simply naughty or rascals, their brains are just not wired to focus or stay put, and that makes it hard for them to perform well in a vast array of situations (school included).

Do not mislabel your child by thinking they are simply naughty or difficult when you may be overreacting to their situation.

If you think that is the case, then enlist the help of a professional who will be able to find out if your child's ADHD affects more of their behavior than you can see. Otherwise, you might end up focusing more on your child's misbehavior than on helping them deal with the root cause of their issues.

## Get Good at Plan B

Parenting, in general, is all about being good at making plans...lots of them, for the same matter. Parenting an explosive child means you must be even better at building plan B, plan C, plan D...and so on. With explosive children, you have to be ready to adjust your plans a great deal, prioritizing what's most important and what could be dealt with easily. At the same time, you also need to make sure that these other plans are not just discarded along the way as it is more likely they will come in handy later. Get good at building contingency plans and build in an unforeseen problem for later.

## Don't Fret Over Disagreements

If your child refuses to eat or throws a tantrum at the dinner table, don't worry about it. They may not be hungry, and they are probably tired. They may want to go to bed or something else and you shouldn't force them to do anything for which they don't wish. Don't insist on disagreeing and constantly fighting with your child -- it won't do them any good, and it will most certainly not benefit you either. Indeed, raising an overly active child can be a challenge, but it does come with a good dose of positives as well. Focus on those whenever times get tough and then roll back your sleeves to be the parent your child needs you to be: one who knows how to guide them through the perpetually distracting world out there.

# Chapter 9:
# Choosing Schools for Explosive Child

Make observation notes and consider your child's learning style and unique personality when selecting schools. Furthermore, please consider your child's behavior as well as his gifts and talents. Look for schools with active support services and a curriculum that matches your child's passions and interests. Furthermore, ensure that you understand the school's policy for dealing with behavioral issues. Set up an interview with the school ahead of time to tour the school and examine the rules and consequences posted on the classroom walls. If possible, get a sense of the school's values and how they handle behavior issues.

There are programs in place for students who have been diagnosed with ADHD, ODD, or CD in public schools. Although each district is unique, all public schools provide IEP and 504 services. On the plus side, public schools offer sports and extracurricular activities. The disadvantage is that there is a high teacher-to-student ratio.

Students with CD and ODD benefit from therapeutic days in schools. Those schools are specifically designed for children who have been diagnosed with behavioral disorders. There, children are educated on social skills. Students return to their district schools once they have learned to produce desired behaviors. Some students, however, may choose to stay for credit recovery purposes.

Private schools may not accept students with behavioral disorders, but they do have smaller classes. Although they benefit from this type of school's structure and strict routine, this student may become frustrated and anxious due to the intense discipline. In this school, impulsive and attention-deficit students are likely to receive detention regularly. The defiant student, on the other hand, may benefit from the structure and strong disciple.

### Charter Schools

Charter schools provide IEPs and 504 plans. They also give the state exam. Charter schools are public schools that are run independently, so each one is unique. Again, it is critical to research the school. The primary focus of one charter school may be behavior management. At the same time, another charter school's primary goal is to improve student achievement. Charter schools typically have a lower teacher-to-student ratio. This type of school may benefit the attention deficit student because it may provide personalized instruction.

## Magnet Schools

The good news is that magnet schools specialize in a specific interest that your child may be interested in. That is a school that may be a good fit for your child's talents and skill set. Students who struggle with behavior may benefit from this type of school because participation increases self-awareness.

## Home School

Homeschooling allows students to be free of the constraints of the classroom. It is advantageous for students who require frequent breaks and freedom, such as impulsive or attention-deficit children. Home school a child with defiant or conduct disorders to train them and then return them to regular school once the desired behavior has been taught.

## Online Virtual School

Most online schools are public schools, which necessitate state testing, IEPs, and 504 plans with testing accommodations. The online school is self-paced, and it may provide personalized instruction and one-on-one virtual learning. This type of school would benefit the defiant student because he would have control over his surroundings. Furthermore, because of the immediate reinforcement after completing each task, this type of instruction is beneficial to the ADHD student. However, highly social students may struggle in this type of school.

## Improving Your Child's Social Skills at Home

The school intervention approach to behavioral therapy for ADHD in children entails assisting teachers in meeting their educational needs by managing ADHD behaviors in the classroom.

Your child's condition makes it difficult for him to learn—he can barely retain a lesson. He may leave his work unfinished because he is either too preoccupied with jumping around the classroom or is too obsessed with tuning out what he should be listening to. And none of this comes as a surprise because the activities your child is required to do in school—listening quietly, sitting still, concentrating, and following instructions—are the same activities they find challenging to do. It is not because they do not want to do a task, but because they cannot do so.

However, with the help of his parents and teachers, your ADHD child has every chance of succeeding in school. Here are some strategies to consider:

Request that your child's teacher:

- Looks for ways to minimize potential distractions in the classroom. It would be preferable to seat children with ADHD, especially those who have difficulty focusing, near the teacher at all times. The teacher may also stand near the student while giving directions; this reduces the number of barriers and distractions the student must overcome to absorb what is being said.
- Makes space for movement. Allow your child to fidget in his seat or move around the classroom by giving them reasons to do so. It would be fantastic to allow children with ADHD to get drinking water, run an errand for the teacher, use the restroom, or complete any other task that requires physical action. A child with ADHD may also be allowed to keep a squeeze ball or another small object in his desk to manipulate without distracting his classmates quietly.
- Makes room for transitions. Request that the teacher reminds your child of an upcoming task or activity, such as recess, the next class, or the time to read another book. It would be ideal if the teacher provided frequent reminders and advance notice for field trips and other special school events. Before the day is over, the teacher may also assist your child in preparing to go home by reminding him of the items he needs to complete his homework.
- Allows for some free time. It allows your child to spend his free time during recess enjoying himself rather than working on a

missed assignment. Playing during his break helps him improve his concentration.

Assist Your Child's Teacher

- Communicate with your child's teacher about his difficulties regularly.
- Assist your child in organizing his papers before doing homework and getting ready for school the following day.
- Check to see if he has completed his homework in complex subjects, especially if he is on the verge of failing a class.
- Request that the teacher uses a daily/weekly report if necessary.
- Check your child's ADHD medication is working as it should while he is at school and doing his homework.
- Make sure your child places his completed homework in the appropriate folder/organizer.
- Save your child's completed homework until the school semester is over.

Make Learning a Pleasurable Experience

- When introducing a lesson in class, use physical motion.
- Make up silly songs to help you remember the details of a new lesson.
- By connecting dry facts to trivia, you can make them more exciting and likely remembered.

Make Math More Fun

- Play games that make numbers enjoyable for your child. You can use dominoes, dice, and memory cards to make math fun for your child, or you can simply wiggle or tuck your fingers in as you help your child add and subtract.
- Make up ridiculous acronyms. These will assist your child in remembering math rules such as operations, divisibility, and so on.
- Create illustrations to help your child understand various mathematical concepts, such as word problems.

Make Reading a Pleasurable Experience

- Read to your child and make the reading time enjoyable for both of you.
- Act out what you just read as a group. Allow your child to choose his favorite character from the story to play. Request that he choose your personality as well. Use costumes and amusing voices to bring the story to life.
- Place wagers with your child. Always ask him how he thinks the story will end. For example, you could say, "The boy in the book sure seems brave; I bet he'll be the one to save the whole town!"

Organizing Your Life

- Create a folder for all your child's completed homework. It would be a good idea to organize open files in color-coded folders and show your child how to file appropriately.
- If possible, keep extra sets of school supplies and textbooks at home.
- Every day, help your child organize his belongings in his backpack, pockets, and folders.
- Teach your child how to create checklists and then assist him in using them. Remind him to cross an item off his list as soon as he completes it.

Getting Homework Done

- Designate a specific time and location for your child to complete his homework. Remove the television, pets, and any other potential distractions.
- Educate your child on the importance of time by using timers and an analog clock. These devices will also allow you to track how well your child completes his homework.
- Allow your child to take a 10- to 20-minute break from homework.

# Chapter 10
# The Parenting Art

Children's conflicts don't begin until they're four, six, or eight, and they may be traced back to reasons long before the events that reveal them. Therefore, parents need to be made aware of this fact. There are several ways parents may come into conflict with their youngsters, including their lackluster nature or unrealistic goals. Parental indifference to the greater obligations of their role as caregivers is a certain predictor of conflict in one or all their children.

We are all responsible for guiding our children toward a life of virtue, not just a life of convenience. The only way to keep children from conflict in the future is to prevent them from becoming money-grubbers, perpetuators of old biases, upholders of false beliefs, or lawless enforcers.

A good rule of thumb for parents is to keep in mind that even the fairest disciplinary measures are often left unsaid. Once, a young man had enormous wealth passed down to him via his mother's side. When this young man attempted to explain to him the potential applications of his resources, he responded as follows: "My parents never stopped telling me what I should not do, and they never taught me what I should be doing. My father has left me with nothing in my life that I owe to him. I've figured out what I shouldn't do now that I've read about it."

When it comes to teaching their children about the dangers of breaking the law and the impossibility of doing so, some parents appear to think that teaching their children these principles is sufficient. The young heir's protest was against this mindset. Simply stating "banned" and "forbidden" will not suffice. Obeying a lengthy list of don'ts does not equate to morality, even if it provides some personal safety. Keep your children out of trouble, but that's not the best outcome if you forbid them to take from others. More must be done to provide them with affirmations of religion and life that inspire lofty goals, genuine standards, and authentic values.

I've heard parents bemoaning a child's misbehavior, saying, "I rarely did or said something bad in front of my children," as if to excuse themselves. This thought process ignores the possibility that youngsters may be unseen, overhearing what isn't stated. However, one can question, did you, by coincidence or purpose, say or do anything positively and persuasively right in front of your child? Many years ago, I observed an incident that has been with me ever since. His dad had just died when his child approached the execution chamber, shook his hand at his deceased father, and said, "You are accountable for the destruction of my existence." Later, I realized that the dad was only a money hoarder who thought he had completed all his responsibilities as a parent since he had given and intended to leave his children a large inheritance.

Parents' primary duty is to be aware of the souls they are allowed to wreck throughout their lifetime. It is fortunate for some parents that most children who see their life in ruins fail to assign blame to the absence of parental moral and spiritual direction. Rather than gathering their words in case their children overhear them, parents should protect their spirits so that their children may observe everything without being distracted. Suppose it is correct that a person's character is revealed with every word he says. In that case, this is especially true in the household, where children listen intently their parents' spoken and unspoken words, and they are ruthless judges of both deeds and words. All our words and actions reflect who we are and what we want our children to believe us to be.

Parents are often reminded to guard their words, but it is also important to be mindful of their actions and well-being. Parental tasks are both good and bad, and it is easy to overlook this when we focus only on the negative aspects of our responsibilities to our children. Of all creatures, parental love and care are the most important.

We must decide whether it is more important to tell children to show respect and reverence for their parents or ask parents if they are worthy of their children's respect. Many years ago, a revered national instructor appealed to the nation's youth to show respect and dignity to their parents. In reality, no one has any right to demand filial regard unless we add a serious request for the elderly to allow the younger to honor and adore them. Do not be so confident that our children are unworthy, but rather question whether we are deserving of the respect and dignity that our parents received from us.

To sum it up, parents must first earn their children's respect by living according to their standards of honor. Children will not respect a father who is only a cash machine, no matter how many wonderful things he buys them. The woman who devotes her life to the unimportant things and stupidities of each season's mandate does not deserve the respect and awe of her children, regardless of the Biblical directives to the contrary. If a father's only concern is the pursuit of material riches and power, his children can't be considered to consider that he is deserving of more than a superficial pat on the wrist and a nod of the head.

To this day, I regret offending a close friend by scolding parents about their failure to earn honor with the same zeal that their children do in return for it. Let's take a closer look at the day-to-day activities of the situation. Could a mom whose life has been devoted to the chase of the useless expect to be revered, even if there comes a moment when she would crave for it and be disappointed that she was unable to get it?

Although there is no danger of future conflict, parents do have a responsibility to offer everything to their offspring, which means to be something to give and to produce something of themselves because then their contribution will be meaningful. And there is no alternative for the gift of oneself, even though one may reward one's efforts in some different ways. There is no way for parents to offer their children a taste of their own experiences. "A child's role is with its mom," calmly said a young lady, the mom of a youngster I was expecting to see with her. The story of the young girl who said she wanted to be a doctor when she grew up so that she could be among her children becomes clearer to those who have seen it.

A child should be with its mother and father. This is contrary to a time when the affluent family felt that a child was best served by a nurse and nanny. Perhaps Abraham Lincoln's mother had it correct. It has always been my opinion that Abraham Lincoln's lack of formal education and the absence of nurses and governesses should not be a cause for concern, since in their place was his mother and the immediateness of her caring presence.

If parental-filial communication isn't direct but rather intermediary, parents can't assist their children to live meaningful lives. Before they understand that a toddler is much more than a body to always be housed and fed and a brain to be equipped and schooled, parents can offer their children anything. It's only when parents realize that their children have souls that they will stop filling their child's bodies with food and cramming their brains with information while neglecting their souls. How frequently, however, do parents lavish attention on their children's lower nature while neglecting their higher one? Because they didn't realize that not only were they co-creators of a child's body but that they were also responsible for its mind and soul.

At the final moment of a friend's farewell, the dad of the boy put a Bible and some Burns poetry in his son's palms and told him to embrace and keep both. If you can't keep the Bible, keep Burns. Are there enough parents who could do the same? To be honest, we can't offer our children much more than clothing, food, and income until we figure out how to produce something of our own.

It is difficult for the influence of the family to climb beyond that of the parents. My son will not bear the hardships that almost destroyed me because I am leaving him well-off, as a parent has said repeatedly. To watch a parent so lovingly raise his child as to convey his deepest desire to help him become a better person is something I've seldom seen. What percentage of parents would want their children to be as well-suited to society as those who want them to be well-suited to themselves?

# Chapter 11:
# Managing an Explosive Child Away from Home

Traveling can be hazardous for a family with an explosive child. If your child goes beyond the bounds and causes damage to the property of others, the consequences could be costly. Even if you do not limit your child's explosive behavior, you risk failing to complete errands and upsetting strangers. It would be fine if self-managed, so how can you make that happen?

As a parent, you are going to need to come up with several action plans for your child. These plans will help them with any struggles or difficulties they encounter because of their disorder symptoms. Whether they are having an outburst at home or a complete meltdown in public, you need to prepare yourself for the possibility that anything can happen at any moment. If one thing is certain, it is that there is nothing certain about the explosive disorder. Your child will also not necessarily be able to tell you when something is about to happen, so you need to pay close attention to their cues.

## Weekends and Vacations

Establishing a schedule for weekends and vacations when the school routine is out is also extremely important. It will be easier for the explosive child if the lack of routine didn't upset the household routine. Schedule time for eating, medications, therapy, sleep, and play. Special classes can be inserted into the routine if needed. Outdoor activities, like hiking or camping, are excellent. During school vacations, don't merely drag your child along on errands or allow him or her to sit bored while you work; that will only make the symptoms worse.

It may not be advisable to take your child to theme parks or museums. Children can act up in museums, especially if they're not designed for young minds. Those where you can only see but not touch will bring out your child's negative symptoms.

On the other hand, amusement parks are generally over-stimulating because of the excessive decorations, lights, and sounds. They are designed to stir the senses, which is not incredibly healthy for your child. However, some amusement parks, like Disneyland and Knott's Berry Farm, allow special passes for children with behavioral disorders. These parks treat such children sensitively, ensuring they don't need to wait in line just to reach the rides.

## Holidays and Events

When your child begins to socialize at school with other children, he or she will begin to receive invitations, such as birthday parties, and it is right that they should attend. Just remember that any event involving your child can raise both their excitement and anxieties, so you must prepare ahead.

When it is time for your own child's party, you should keep it low-key. You don't need to compete in the biggest party contests, as some parents do at this age. Just invite your child's closest friends and take them out for ice cream. Nor should you allow yourself to get stressed by the annual holiday seasons. You don't have to hang up as many lights and decorations as your neighbors. Just stick to the essential family rituals, like a special dinner and opening presents together.

## Tips for Traveling with Young Children

Traveling with adolescents for an extended timeframe requires more than purchasing airfare and reserving hotel rooms. This is especially valid if the get-away goal will be new to everybody traveling.

Guardians should be prepared to manage the unforeseen. Additional tolerance and a comical inclination are musts on any outing with children. Cleverness can defuse numerous upsetting circumstances.

Coming up next are tips that help make a family get-away a triumph:

- Pack snacks. You don't need your little ones to eat sugary treats before flying since sugar can build a child's anxiety and irritability and disturb rest schedules.
- Allow enough time for several restroom visits preceding boarding.

- Bring workbooks to kill time. Tablets and shading books can demonstrate to give valuable interruptions.
- When boarding, urge your children to locate their seats.
- Stress the significance of keeping their seatbelts on.
- If this is your child's first flight, depict how taking off will feel before boarding and clarify how at some point flights hit choppiness.
- Choose lodgings that offer free Continental breakfast if possible. This not only saves money but also eases the stress of finding something to eat each morning.
- Find a neighborhood supermarket so you can buy your child's recognizable snacks for day trips and lodging.
- Map out where you will be venturing out in front of time.

## Traveling with Your Explosive Child

The new relationship you develop with your child will be highly beneficial wherever you go, but unusual issues may arise during car rides. Driving when your child is misbehaving is both aggravating and dangerous. You may be in a hurry at times, and if your child refuses to assist, they will disrupt the schedule.

You want your child to put on a seat belt without prompting, but they may refuse if upset about something else. It makes more sense to investigate the source of the child's annoyance rather than focusing solely on lack of compliance. Because the back seat can be lonely, being proactive can help you avoid unwanted attention. You can include your child in a conversation, pack items of interest, or play a game with them to make the trip less lonely and boring.

You may be concerned about your child if he or she causes a commotion while driving and you may need to pull over until you can get the situation under control. Yes, you may be late, but it is your best option. Remind your child that you can only drive while everyone is seated and buckled in. However, make sure the children stop fighting and do something else, even if it's just looking out the window. Fighting can resume fast if they are not distracted from the conflict.

When there is constant disagreement over the seating arrangements in the car, apply the same techniques that you would use to minimize conflict within the household; help the children figure out the sharing system they want to use. Do this before your next trip; ask the children if they have any suggestions to fix the problem when everyone is calm. Every child may have a unique seating choice, but if the children find out what works for them, everything will be fine. Ensure that everyone knows the plan beforehand. It allows them to prepare for what's to come and minimizes surprises.

Problems in the Store

Your child may be very cooperative if you are looking for something they enjoy. However, when they feel compelled to buy for others, their actions may be markedly different. As is often the case, when they lack the authority to decide what happens, your child's explosive behavior is sparked and intensified.

If you're in a good mood, your child will behave better, which gives you a lot of power. Talking about your child's favorite topics of conversation can also help make unnecessary shopping less annoying. Most importantly, if your child understands what is going on, he or she is more likely to comply. For example, if you're going grocery shopping, you could ask her if she wants to help you decide what to buy. Older children may be willing to assist you in your search for bargains. Others may wish to read the grocery list or push the cart.

Public Misbehavior

Unfortunately, if a child's behavior becomes disrespectful or dangerous, you may be forced to stop your child or leave the store physically. In some cases, you may be able to re-enter the store after a short time if your child calms down and you are confident that everything will be fine when you return.

However, you might have to return later without your child. Your child must understand that their actions have repercussions. In these circumstances, you can demonstrate such negative consequences. To begin, you may say, "Because we haven't finished our shopping, we'll have to return later, and I won't be able to make the dessert I was planning for tonight." If the problem persists, you may want to take it a step further. You could suggest that your child use some of their own money to pay for the return trip, emphasizing the benefits of this option (e.g., this compensates others for inconveniencing them and might mitigate their complicated feelings against them). Everyone benefits when they offer reimbursement.

As with hygiene issues described in the beginning, you could also ask your child if they want to stay home the next time and use some of their own money to hire someone to keep them company. As a result, they bear some of the burdens of refusing to comply with the family plan. Offer them options but let them know that some of them may come at a cost.

Relationship with non-family members

Is your child accusing other children of gaining a sense of superiority? Is your child attempting to buy friends by giving away personal items while demonstrating low self-esteem? Should he complain about being mistreated to get you to defend? Will he always sit alone on the playground, or will he only play with children outside the standard circle?

If any of these are true, consider changing things up to prevent this from happening. You want your child to have a fun social life and to feel comfortable interacting with a wide range of people.

When your child meets another rambunctious child, his behavior likely becomes exaggerated as a child with explosive disorder. If he behaves stupidly and doesn't try to meet standards, he stops feeling inferior, and there is no loss when he plays with another volatile child. There is strength in numbers, and when your child joins forces with a "bad friend," he gains influence and leverage.

You can try to keep your child away from other disruptive children. However, it may give your child the impression that he or she is weak and easily manipulated. Another approach is to help them understand why they are incorrect and assist them in successfully dealing with negative influences. This approach gives them the impression that they will show up and affect change in their environment. They will regard themselves as a wise leader. "Your friend might be clever enough to imitate you when you're playing together," you might say.

If your child is young, he will most likely mimic many of the behaviors he observes in other adults in the family. If he is demanding and possessive with you, he may also be challenging and possessive with his playmates. When family members manipulate or mistreat him, he may overreact or exhibit fear. For these reasons, it is critical to cultivate habits that are compatible with non-family members. Improve his ability to connect within the group if you want him to communicate, accept social boundaries, and interact assertively with his peers.

Exercise

Most forms of exercise help to sharpen attention, promote learning, and improve social skills. Encourage your children to exercise. Let them go swimming, biking, or jogging. Let them dance, run, or play soccer. Take them backpacking so they can enjoy the beauty of nature.

Children benefit in varied ways when they engage in regular exercise. They interact with other children. They have fun. They stay healthy. They have self-confidence. Aside from providing these benefits, regular exercise generates other effects that have a positive impact on a child who has explosive disorders.

A child with explosive disorder is impulsive, unfocused, or hyperactive. They are edgy and fidgety. They seem to be in perpetual motion; they chatter incessantly, squirm, run around, and are generally restless and unfocused.

Exercise helps control these symptoms. It helps a child harness his energy. It gives him a target, something to focus their energy and attention on. It helps them stay focused and motivated.

Exercise controls aggression. It provides an outlet for excess energy. It helps improve your child's mood. It makes them less anxious and less cranky throughout the day.

Exercise also helps your child sleep better at night. A healthy level of physical exhaustion induces deep sleep which is beneficial for your child.

# Chapter 12:
# Improving Social Skills of Explosive Children

## How to Identify Challenges in Social Skills

According to research, children with explosive disorders have social problems that include strained relationships with their classmates, trouble establishing and retaining friends, and deficits in proper social conduct. Long-term outcome studies show that these issues persist into adolescence and adulthood, obstructing individuals with this disorder social adjustment.

Suggestions for spotting challenges:

- Look around you for hints to assist you in interpreting the subtext. Keep an eye out for more alternatives.
- To better understand what someone is saying, pay attention to their tone of voice, body language, demeanor, or the expression in their eyes.
- To better discern the subtext, look at a person's choice of words. ("I would love to go" is most likely a yes.) "If you want to" implies that they probably aren't interested but will do it anyhow.)

Words are less effective than actions. If someone's words indicate one thing, but their actions suggest another, it is a good idea to think about if their actions reflect their sentiments.

Explosive children very often may have problems with rules and socialization, with their peers at school (during breaks in particular), or on the playground.

Below are some common situations and suggestions to help children deal with them.

Children with behavioral disorders, because they are often considered clumsy and impulsive, can be the target of bullying. Mind you, bullying is different from teasing because it is a repeated act, it is a subversive system that often escalates over time. It can include name-calling, threats, exclusion, and even physical violence.

Therefore, how to help?

First, talk about it. Explain what bullying is and make sure the child knows they can talk to their parent or teacher about it if they experience it or see it.

Explain that he can leave the situation if he doesn't feel safe, or if using words to defend himself doesn't work. Remind them that responding with insults to other insults can throw gasoline on the fire.

Being Overly Aggressive with Other Children or Classmates

Explosive children sometimes totally lack impulse-control and have trouble filtering what they say. They may physically push other children simply because they dislike something about them, run around inattentively, or call others unkind names. It is also possible that they may not realize their strength.

So, what needs to be done?

It is critical to set and explain the ground rules well at home to avoid physical aggression so that the child knows the consequences beforehand. Encourage using words instead of one's body to communicate.

Before entering the park, for example, it's helpful to remind your child that being hit, or wounded, can hurt a lot...but also the importance of asking with words before taking, waiting your turn, and apologizing.

Often it is not enough for them to explain it with words alone, you might simulate some situations at home and repeat them together, to make sure they have understood (role play).

Not Wanting to Play with Other Children

Being on the playground involves learning social skills explosive children lack, including sharing, taking turns, and knowing how to converse.

The child may not be sure how to start a conversation, fit into a small group of other children, or how to ask to participate in a game. He or she may not understand when other children are inviting him or her to play. This can make it difficult to develop friendships.

How to help them make distinctions?

Again, practice this at home. It is particularly useful to simulate introductions, suggesting some examples: "Hello, I'm Paolo, what's your name?" or perhaps: "Would you like to play ball with me?" "Please, may I join you?"

It will be important to explain to the child that sometimes it is not possible to participate in a game that is already in progress and organized without asking explicitly how to do it (simulation), which is not obvious to him.

## Effect of Explosive Disorder on Peer Relationships

When a child hosts a birthday party and none of the children who were invited show up, it is upsetting not only for the child but also for the parent. Parents want to see their children laughing and having fun with their peers, and it is never easy when they are isolated.

It is not like children do not want to make friends; they do, but they just do not know how to do it. Sometimes it is not always the other children's fault that they will not associate with your child, but their parents may have a hand in that. For example, teens who have no sense of danger may persuade their peers to skip school. The parent of the child who does not have the condition will undoubtedly warn their adolescent to stay away from the "troubled child." There are numerous things a parent can do to prevent this from happening. However, before that, parents must understand how explosive affects the child's relationship with their peers.

Express Impatience by Not Waiting Their Turn

Explosive children are very impatient as has been proven in previous cases. It does not exactly bond well with your peers if you keep cutting them in line. Children are impatient tiny people, but they are trained to practice the art. A child with a behavioral disorder does not have the sense to be patient and will find themselves cutting others in the line.

Assume that a child has been waiting in line for sweets when another child cuts them in line and ends up getting the candy; when it is their turn, their candy is gone. Of course, the child will not blame the adult for not bringing enough candy but will remember that the reason they did not get one was because of another child who couldn't wait if they could.

This resentment from the children is unlikely to encourage them to befriend the child with the explosive disorder. It is even more difficult to persuade them that it was not the child's fault. How do you explain to a group of 12-year-olds that the behavioral child explosions did not cause the mishap on purpose when they witnessed it? While you can explain away a behavior to other adults and have them understand, this is not the same case with children. So, in this case, it is the explosive child that needs guidance. You will need to guide them on how to approach certain situations, so they don't end up annoying and hurting their peer's feelings, thus developing a negative reputation among them.

Talk Over Their Peers

Explosive children battle with concentration. They talking over others is viewed as a sign of disrespect, and other children do not take too kindly to it. Sometimes, those children do this to keep their focus on the conversation as they have a short attention span. Talking and listening need active participation, and it is easier for those children to talk than to listen. This is because their short attention span does not allow them to stay focused on the same thing for a long time.

Have a Difficult Time Paying Attention to Others

This comes back to them having a short attention span. Imagine having a conversation with someone, sharing something with them only to find they are not paying attention to you. And to make it worse, they missed almost the whole conversation. This is going to, without a doubt, make you angry—especially when you listen when it is their turn, and the least, they can do for you is pay attention.

Unlike teens who also encounter this problem, they do not exactly understand that this is an effect of a condition. Explaining this to a child may be difficult, and besides, it is the child with the condition who requires assistance because a parent will not always be present in all their child's interactions to explain away the behavior.

Get Jealous of the Other Children

When the child wants to make friends, this is not the right attitude to have. If they are in art class working on something that needs all their focus, this child will grow resentful that the other children remained focused on their work, enough to finish it on time and receive commendation from the teacher. They can't be friends if they hate the other person for things that are beyond their control.

Parents must understand that if they do not help their children acknowledge and accept their situation, first by leading by example, the child will grow to despise what they are and those who have what is beyond their means. Being envious of other children can be relatively harmless, but it must be stopped before it becomes so.

Like to Be the Center of Attention

Explosive children who are hyperactive frequently perform dangerous stunts to impress their peers. It is sometimes necessary to make a statement such as, "Look, I can do this better than you." As a way of proving themselves and making amends for their shortcomings. For example, a student may be having difficulty focusing on a class assignment, and the teacher continues to call them out in front of the entire class, embarrassing them. This child will feel the need to draw attention to themselves and distance themselves from the other thing they are unable to do. That thing on which the other children are fixated. They may play dangerous pranks on other students or get into fights over trivial matters to demonstrate to you that they are more than that one thing they can't do and that what they can do, they can do better than you.

## Parents Role in Helping Their Children Make Friends

Explosive children may appear insensitive to the feelings of others, unsure of what to say or how to act when confronted with situations in which their response is expected, and not just any response, but one that has a positive impact. It is not enough to simply tell the child how to behave; you must also demonstrate how to do so. Here is how you can do it.

Say your child had a conversation with their peer at school where the other child was talking about how they were having problems with a math assignment. Just a simple conversation, however, it goes on longer than it usually would because the other child breaks out into details of the work. This is already enough to have the explosive child grow bored. As far as we know about behavioral disorders, we realize two things might happen in this particular case. Those children may interrupt the conversation, bring up a whole different topic, and thus make the other feel dismissed, or the child will just zone off and start daydreaming which has the same result as the first.

Control the Environment

Picking a safe environment for your child, whether they have an explosive disorder or not is important. Look at the place you are taking your child to study and play with other children. The daycare that you take your child off to. Are they in an environment surrounded by people that are sensitive to mental health issues or are they willing to learn and adjust accordingly?

What parents need to understand is that the environment in which you send your child is important because this influences them. The people around you can help or hurt your child's mental health. For example, a school where children learn about mental health and how it affects others. When your child is zoning out during a conversation, they do not take it personally and do everything they can to refocus their attention on the topic at hand. This is not to say that the children must like or tolerate when explosion symptoms manifest in situations, but they understand and are unwilling to let it affect their relationship with the child.

Be an Example

Children learn by example. What you do is what they'll find themselves doing and that's why sometimes people use the words, "You take after your mother" or "Your father would have done the same thing." All this starts at an early age and the habits stick into their teenage years that follow them into adulthood.

When it comes to friends—the kind you have, how you treat them, and they treat you, in turn, does not go unnoticed to the child. Do you sit around and talk about that friend who is not around, say mean things about them, and then pretend all that did not happen when they come? Do you go to them when they are in trouble, and do they come to your aid when something goes wrong on your end?

Sign Them Up for Social Groups

This is where you assist your child. Children with explosive disorder thrive in social settings, as opposed to children with depression or social anxiety who prefer it when left to their own devices. It's not that they don't want to make friends; they just don't know how to do it. How do they get these children to like them and want to hang out with them?

This not only helps them make friends, but it also teaches them new skills. Assume you sign them up for a music class in which they must collaborate with other children. Playing a musical instrument requires concentration, but it is also a changing and repetitive activity. Repetitiveness is beneficial because it allows them to become experts in one area and provides a pattern for them to follow. Because they will not always play the same thing all the time, the art remains interesting.

Keep In Contact with Their Caregivers

Parents with explosive children need to keep in contact with their caregivers or teachers. When the child's babysitter understands the child's condition, they get in a better position to help the child. Assume that the teacher at your children's school understands the child's condition and recognizes that they lose focus in class, making it difficult for them to focus on their work; they also recognize that the child has learning difficulties. They will not address the children's issues in front of the rest of the class, which will embarrass them.

Arrange Playdates for the Children

Invite your friend's children over and arrange playdates. Most of the time, family friends run in families where the children are friends because their parents are friends. What better person is there than the one who has been with you and does not require you to explain your child's condition because they have been there the entire journey? By extension, their child comprehends the situation. Playdates with other children and encouraging sleepovers help the children bond.

When parents and children spend time together, they form bonds. For example, when you organize play dates for your child, they can share and discover what they have in common, allowing the conversations to be light and the child not to have to try too hard.

Ease Your Child into Social Settings

Explosive children already have self-esteem issues and are afraid of others' rejection because of what they already know. Using the previous example, where the children in their class are already aware that this child has learning difficulties, their self-esteem is already crushed, how do you as a parent ease your child into the social setting, especially when they are reluctant to do so? Easing a child into a social setting mostly entails the step you take before you let them interact with others and they may include:

Talk about the Issues You Encounter When Presented with a Situation like Theirs

Help them understand that there is no such thing as a perfect friend and tell them the challenges you encountered when it came to making friends in their age and ways in which you encounter the issues to date. This way, they won't feel so bad about themselves when it doesn't work out in the long run. They will understand that sometimes friendships work and sometimes they just don't.

In a social setting, parents should refrain from speaking for their children because you are not assisting them. You must remember that you will not always be with that child. Trying to explain their condition instead of allowing the child to try on their own is not helping them. You must allow them to make mistakes for them not to repeat them.

## How to Help Your Child Make Friends

- Congratulate them. When they do have successful interactions, congratulate your child. Watch them closely when they play with other children so you can always keep a watchful eye and monitor the situation; they are in. You can intervene if there is a fight if your child starts telling fibs or if they are trying to attempt something dangerous to impress their friends.

- Try not to dive in. When introducing a new sport to your explosive child, speak with the coach first before going in for the first practice. Ask questions about whether your child who has the explosive disorder is welcomed in the team. You can follow your child to meet the instructor, who may introduce your child to the game a little bit before the first practice.
- Take note of their competitive attitude explosive children can also have difficulty in competitive play. Gloating on winning and crying on losing. If your child experiences these circumstances with difficulty, get them to learn other kinds of athletic abilities that do not require doing it as a team, such as martial arts, running, gymnastics, golfing, and cycling.
- Trust that they will find their way. Children will eventually learn to cope and handle their situations and behaviors better, even when they have experienced social isolation. They will also learn how friendships work. When a child hits adolescence, they will act on the urge to fit in.
- Having just a few friends. This is something that needs to be drilled into the child. They do not need to be part of a huge group of friends or be invited into plenty of parties to be happy. Studies show that having close friends is what is needed for a child to be happy, to be socially developed, and to have self-confidence.
- Find a mentor. Having a peer who acts as a big brother or big sister can be extremely helpful as they are more likely to take advice or instructions from them than from a parent. You can ask an elder sibling to become an informal mentor to your child. Many schools offer mentorship programs so you can ask your school if they can connect your child to a peer.
- Follow the love. Your child may already be interested in a certain sport or a video game. If they already have developed an interest in a specific game or skill, help them connect with an interest group as this will help your child feel confident, engaged, and belong.
- One-on-one play. Playdates with one child can prove to be extremely helpful for children to learn social cues. You can add on two children to the playdate, but more than that may seem overwhelming, and your explosive disorders child may like they are being attacked.
- Set good examples. Teaching your child the best ways to act and react in social situations, will help them make that same

- determination to form and create friendships with the children of your friends too.
- Take teasing head-on bullying, playful banter and teasing are all the inevitable elements of childhood and friendships. Explosive children may not be able to respond correctly, so parents are advised to help the child maneuver through the teasing and harassment they face by standing up to their bullies, not overreacting, and seeking out an adult's help at any time.
- Keep playdates short. For children aged 10 or under, it's probably best for playtime to be less.
- Getting the dosage right. Puberty is a good period to relook the dosage and medication given to your child. As puberty hits, your child will go through all sorts of hormone changes in their body. Often things that worked before puberty may not have the same effect anymore.
- Observe your child. When they are playing with other children, sit back and observe. You can learn a lot about how your child socializes if you just watch how they play. Pay attention to when they get frustrated and what sets them off. Most of the time, explosive children are a lot more prone to frustration and having outbursts than the average child. Try not to insert yourself too much.
- Believe they will find their way. You need to let your child make mistakes and do what they feel is instinctually right. Even if they mess up, they are learning. If they are not hurting themselves or anyone else, you need to step back to allow them to grow.

## Helping Your Child Improve Their Social Skills

Simple social interactions prove to be another hurdle for explosive children. These difficulties are such as talking too much or not being able to read social cues, interrupting frequently, or just coming off as too intense or aggressive. Because they mature differently from their peers, those children can be a subject of teasing and bullying. Despite their emotional immaturity, they are gifted with an acute sense of creativity and intelligence. Often, they figure out ways of coping or getting along with other children or even spot people who are not friends. Their personality traits can sometimes exasperate parents as well as teachers, but sometimes to their peers, it can be funny and charming.

Social skills and rules can be a hurdle for explosive disorder children. In this area, you can help them become better listeners or even become better at reading people's faces and body language when they interact with their peers.

Show them how to make changes with their behavior by speaking gently and honestly to them about their challenges.

Help your child through various scenarios by doing some role-play to make learning social skills fun. Choose playmates that have similar abilities and language capacities as your child, so they do not feel out of place.

At first, invite just one or two friends. Pay attention while they are playing and have a policy of zero tolerance to hit, push and scream.

During a child's development phase, some skills are quantifiable language skills, math skills, etc.

But what about the softer skills which, like social skills, do not come as naturally? Explosive children also find it difficult to make friends and establish relationships. Some parents wonder how social skills can be developed, but often don't know where to start.

All children must have positive peer relationships and friendships. However, most explosive children have a hard time making friends and being included in a wider group of peers. Oftentimes, hyperactivity, inattention as well as impulsiveness can disrupt a child's attempt at connecting with the people around them positively. Not feeling belonging, not being accepted, feeling different, isolated, and unlikeable is, unfortunately, the painful feelings explosive children go through, and this experience carries on into adulthood, often with lasting and disastrous effects on their future attempts at making friends and forming connections. Explosive children are no different than children without all of them wanting to be liked, want to be part of a group, and want to make friends, they just do not know how to do it.

## Increasing a Child's Social Awareness

According to various research on explosive disorders, children with this condition can be low monitors of their social behavior. They often do not have clarity, awareness, or understanding of social situations and the reactions they provoke from people around them.

An explosive child's interaction with a peer may have gone well, but it did not. It is another example of an explosions-disorder related issue. According to the social setting, they cannot accurately read social situations, self-monitor themselves, and adjust their actions and behaviors accordingly. These skills must be taught directly to them.

Teach Skills Directly and Practice, Practice, Practice

Learning from past experiences also makes it a little more challenging when it comes to explosive children. They often react without thinking, but one way to remedy this would be to continually provide feedback immediately whenever a child's behavior is inappropriate due to social miscues. Role-play is a beneficial way of shaping, teaching, and practicing positive social skills and providing the child with ways to deal with difficult situations, such as bullying and teasing.

# Chapter 13:
# Understand the Factor that Contribute to Challenging Episodes

The biological foundation that contributes to explosiveness may stem from the genes possessed by an individual which in turn affects their personality, development, upbringing, and social experiences or learning experiences. It is more likely that those who have the highest levels of impulsivity and aggression will also develop incendiary personality. The biological foundation that contributes to explosiveness is assumed to be the effect of the interplay between the behavioral and neurological influences, which together affect children's personality development in the early years. The whole concept of explosive behavior is based on a predisposition to mental-behavioral problems and this predisposition is usually associated with territorial aggression that generally leads to an explosive episode. In most cases, it is believed that biological risk factors (e.g., impulsivity and aggression) contribute to both mental disorders as well as reactive aggressive behaviors. It has been found that some of the child's natural predispositions for explosion is rooted in their early developmental experiences, which have a direct link to their destructive behaviors. It has been noted that many children exposed to event that were traumatic or physically or emotionally stressful in their early years will often display aggressive behavior and may be out of control. The biological factors that contribute to explosive behavior can be a result of a child's inability to process their thoughts, feelings and behaviors in an appropriate and constructive manner. The nature of some of the thoughts, feelings or behaviors is often linked to the child's inability to cope with their environment, or their internal reactions or feelings.

Parents play a vital role in contributing to the explosive behavior. A parent can significantly contribute to the explosive behavior development in a child due to their negative parenting style and inappropriate discipline techniques. Because parents often do not understand their own behaviors or the factors that bring out their worst parenting style, they are often unaware of how they contribute substantially towards explosive behavior in young children. The role of the parents in contributing to an explosive child is especially significant if the parents do not have a better understanding of their own emotions and feelings and therefore do not allow such feelings to be expressed.

For example, when a parent becomes irritated with their child, they may not know how to express themselves properly or how to manage their anger in a constructive way. When they find it difficult to manage the explosive emotions they feel, these emotions will result in varying levels of aggression which may be directed towards those close to them. If the parents do not understand how to deal with their emotions, and/or they become frustrated with the child's behavior, they may resort to negative, aggressive or manipulative behaviors which may exacerbate the turmoil or frustration they feel.

A child's environment can also be a factor that affects their explosiveness. If a child is exposed to negative or aggressive behaviors at home or at school, they will usually act out the same behavior. If there are instances of abuse or violence in the family, the child will be more likely to act out the same behavior as they grow up. The child's environment can also include the various influences that happen within the classroom and at school, such as peer groups, violence on television and graphic images which are linked to violent events. The child's environment may also include their educational experiences, in which the influence of the social group and their classmates on their behavior can also serve as a catalyst for explosive episodes.

## Effects of Marriage and Divorce on Your Children Emotional Health

Divorce can cause children to regress emotionally. When a child's parents are divorced, it is believed that they can experience a higher risk of emotional problems than when their parents are not divorced. Children who have experienced the divorce of their parents will usually be more likely to develop problems such as depression and anxiety, which have been linked with an increased propensity for aggressive behaviors. A common emotional reaction to a divorce occurs when the children feel guilty for some of their actions that have led to the divorce. Anger and resentment towards one parent may also be present, as well as a feeling of loneliness or insecurity when not living with both parents. Children are often afraid to express the emotions that they are feeling, and this can lead to further emotional problems.

Emotional problems may also occur if a child is not brought up in harmony with their biological parents. Children who are not brought up in the same household as their birth parents may experience confusion and uncertainty about their feelings. When children do not know how to relate to one parent, they can develop emotional problems, especially when they do not feel accepted by both parents. Children are often confused about expressing their emotions, which leads to issues that may create a sense of anxiety or frustration that they communicate through aggressive behavior. Children may also experience confusion when they do not know how to relate to one parent. When there are issues with the custody of the children, it can create a feeling of uncertainty for the child.

Children who are raised in such a manner, or have experienced a divorce, will often struggle in learning to express their emotions appropriately, and therefore may resort to destructive behaviors. Children exposed to divorce are usually left without guidance due to the lack of communication and understanding between parents. The use of aggressive techniques by both parents can exacerbate existing emotional problems. A child may notice the aggressive behaviors they see in their parents, and they will usually develop problems relating to their own aggression.

The parent-child relationship is further impacted by parental divorce. Children will generally begin to distrust the adults around them, especially after a failed marriage. They will usually feel abandoned by one or both parents and experience feelings of abandonment, rejection, or low self-esteem when they are unable to see both parents. Children may develop a feeling of hatred towards their parents as they look for someone to take the blame for the divorce. The child will then begin to act out in aggressive and destructive ways. Emotional problems can lead to a diminished ability to cope with stressful events, which can result in increased explosive behaviors.

## Help the children see why he/she is upset

With a child in distress, it is important that you can speak their language. If your child is upset because they were not invited to a birthday party, they may be struggling with the social aspect of seeing their friends again. It might appear that your child was sent home from school earlier than planned and wanted to show their frustration at seeing the other students enjoying themselves. Empathizing with your child will allow them to understand their emotions and explain what is causing these feelings of anger or disappointment.

Explain the problem

When your child is upset or in a state of distress, it is important that they understand why they feel that way. Explain to them why they are being sent home early or why their friends were invited to a party, and they were not. This will help them pinpoint exactly what it is that makes them feel upset and angry. Helping your child identify their feelings will also help you understand what exactly caused the problem in the first place.

Encourage them to use their words

If your child is feeling frustrated or angry, they may need to be encouraged to express their feelings to find a solution. After explaining the situation and understanding why they are upset or angry, encourage them to think of ways in which the issue can be resolved. It is important that you listen carefully to what your child says and try to understand where they are coming from. Encourage them to use non-violent ways of expressing their feelings and emotions if needed.

Explain the consequences

When your child is feeling frustrated or angry, you should encourage them to think about the consequences of their actions. For instance, if your child is extremely angry about being sent home early from school for misbehaving, explain to them that this may lead to them being sent home earlier than planned again. If your child's friends were invited to a party, help you child realize that their behavior was the reason they did not receive an invitation.

Explain to them in a nice way why their behavior is not acceptable

Once your child has calmed down, explain to them why their behavior is not acceptable. If your child was sent home from school because they were extremely angry, explain to them that this is a sign that they cannot control their feelings and it may affect their future at school. By helping your child understand exactly why their actions or attitude are not acceptable, they will be able to take the steps needed to resolve the problem.

Use positive reinforcements

Teach your child how to deal with frustration and anger through positive reinforcements. This will help them to understand that there are many ways in which they can manage their feelings when they are angry or frustrated. For example, if your child was sent home from school because they were not able to control their feelings, you can explain to that this is an opportunity to learn something new and gain self-confidence.

Explain to your child why it is important that they learn how to deal with their feelings positively

Explain to your child why it is so important that they learn how to manage their emotions. They need to see that it is vital that they do so and understand how this can affect their everyday life. For example, your child was sent home from school for being extremely upset about being sent home early on a previous occurrence for not controlling their anger. Explain to your child that this may affect their future at school, so it is important that they learn how to control their emotions and learn to manage their emotions in more positive ways.

Remove distractions

Children find it difficult to focus on what they are doing when they are frustrated or angry. To help them deal with their feelings in a more effective fashion, remove distractions to help them stay focused on the task at hand. For example, your child was sent home from school because they were not able to control their anger. You could remove all other distractions when you are close to your child, such as the television or a mobile phone to help them complete the classwork need to complete without becoming distracted.

Help your child communicate with emotions

When children are agitated or angry, it may be difficult for them to communicate their feelings. In these situations, you will have to talk them through it to help them understand why they are experiencing these feelings. It can also help them to resolve the issue that is causing the problem in the first place. For example, your child was sent home from school because they didn't control their anger. If they remain angry, they may get into more fights or even create other problems at school.

Help them to talk about the problem

Once you notice that your child is unable to control their behavior, help them to understand why they are behaving in this way. This would help them understand the problem and help them resolve it in a more successful manner. For example, your child was sent home from school because he was not able to control his anger or frustration. You should encourage your child to talk about their feelings, which could help them understand why they were feeling angry.

Ask questions

For them learn, you should always encourage them to ask questions and discuss things. This would help your child to learn from their mistakes and be aware of the consequences of their actions. For example, if your child was sent home from school for a failure to control their emotions, encourage them to ask you questions about why they were no longer welcome at school. This will help them understand that their actions can have serious consequences, which could help them in future situations.

# Chapter 14:
# Basic Principles for Dealing with an Explosive and Angry Child

If you're a parent, you've almost certainly dealt with an angry child. We frequently end up in yelling battles with our children, or we freeze up, unsure what to do when an angry outburst arises. Anger is a typical emotion in both children and adults. However, how we express and cope with our anger is the difference between living in relative calm and feeling at our wits' end.

Learning to manage angry children and teenagers is a lifelong process and a vital skill to master. Continue reading to learn our top ten rules for coping with an angry child.

### Don't yell at or challenge your child when he or she is angry.

Parents frequently respond to their children's angry outbursts by confronting them and screaming back. However, this will just exacerbate your sense of being out of control. In a crisis, the greatest thing you can do is be cool.

Consider this: even if you are in a vehicle accident and the other motorist is upset at you, if you can remain cool, they will likely relax and be reasonable. However, if you respond aggressively, saying, "What are you talking about, that was your fault," the tension will remain elevated.

So, if your youngster is angry, don't question him. That only adds fuel to the flames. Instead, be patient and wait for him to settle down.

### Avoid attempting to reason with your child during an angry outburst.

When their children are angry, many parents I speak with resort to reasoning. After all, as adults, we employ logic to diffuse heated situations. However, reasoning with an angry child is often difficult since they do not have the same ability as we must pause and reason.

So, while dealing with your angry child, you must leave that linguistic space where you feel most at ease and employ a variety of tactics. "Why are you furious at me?" he asks. "You were the one who forgot your homework at school," will only aggravate your youngster. Instead, wait till he calms down and then discuss it later.

## Be Aware of Your Reactions

It's critical to keep an eye on your reactions, both physical and emotional. "Yikes, I'm in the presence of someone who is highly upset," your senses will warn you. The adrenaline begins pumping through your system and your heart will begin to beat quicker.

However you may feel on the inside, outwardly, you will have to exude an attitude of calm. Remember that you are providing your strength to your children during these difficult times. You are teaching children how to deal with rage by remaining cool and by remaining cool, you are not engaging in a power struggle.

Paying attention to your reactions can also help your youngster focus on himself since he will not have to worry about you or your feelings. If you do not answer gently, your child will intensify his tantrum to attract your attention. To manage an outburst swiftly and successfully, you'll need to draw on some excellent parenting abilities.

## Do Not Engage in Physical Contact with Your Child

In our online parent counseling sessions, we occasionally hear from parents who have lost their cool and been physically abusive to their children. I received a call from a parent whose teenage child yelled at his mother and was shoved by the father. The altercation became more heated.

Following that, the son refused to speak to his father because he believed his father owed him an apology. The father, on the other hand, believed that his child was to blame for the situation and was concerned that apologizing would undermine his authority. "I lost control and it was terrible for me to shove you. I sincerely sorry," I told him to say. Nothing more. That concludes the narrative. We all make errors from time to time, and when we do, we apologize, make amends, and move on.

Do not discuss your child's participation in that event since it is an attempt to blame someone else for your conduct. Instead, you want to educate your child how to accept responsibility and apologize sincerely.

Don't worry, you'll have more opportunity to work with your youngster on being mouthy or disobedient in the future. However, it is critical to be a good role model and confront your involvement in the fight's demise. Remember that becoming violent with your child, among other things, teaches him to address his issues with aggressiveness.

## Use a Different Approach with Younger Children

If your little child (aged eighteen months to four years) is having a temper tantrum, you should step away from him but not entirely isolate him. When tiny children are distressed, you should assist them understand that they can play a role in calming themselves down. You might say:

"I wish I could help you calm down." "Perhaps you might lie down on the couch for a while."

Tell them to relax until they feel in control. You're urging them to pay attention to themselves by doing so. Instead of saying, "You have to wait there for 10 minutes by yourself," say, "When you feel better and are no longer sad, you may come on out and join us."

You may also provide them with an option. "Do you need time to go into your room and get yourself together?" you may ask.

Again, don't test them when they're in that state.

## Don't Panic When Your Child Has a Tantrum

When their children have tantrums or start yelling at them, some parents freeze. The parent is emotionally overwhelmed and either gets immobilized by indecision or succumbs to the child's demands.

If this describes you, you may notice that your child will become angry on purpose to engage you. They'll bait you by throwing a fit or saying something offensive in the hopes that you'll cave. Don't fall for the bait. Don't become angry or give in.

In some of these cases, I believe parents may bargain with their children. Often, parents struggle to manage their own emotions, and as a result, they are unable to adequately train their child at the time. But keep in mind that if you give in and bargain, even occasionally, you're teaching your child that it's worthwhile to act out. Allow your child to calm down and attempt to coach him to apply his problem-solving abilities later.

When you refuse to negotiate, you are not, in my opinion, being passive. On the contrary, you are intentionally choosing not to engage in a debate. "I'm not going to bargain," you declare. "I'm going to remain cool." On the surface, it may not appear so, yet those options are actions.

## Impose Consequences for Bad Behavior, Not Anger

When your child has a temper tantrum, starts screaming, and loses it, make sure you give him consequences based on his behavior rather than his emotions.

For example, if your youngster curses at you during his angry outburst, give him a punishment afterwards for swearing. But if all he does is storm into his room and shout about how unfair life is, let him go. Anger is a normal emotion, and children experience it in the same way that adults do. They must believe that they have a safe place to vent their frustrations.

Children should be allowed to feel angry if they are not breaking any rules or being rude.

## Avoid using excessively harsh punishments.

Punishing someone harshly in the heat of the moment is a lost endeavor. Consider this: Assume your child is angry. He's throwing a temper tantrum, yelling and screaming at you. "If you don't get it together, I'm going to take away your phone for a week," you keep repeating. Okay, it's now been two weeks. Keep it up...been it's a month. "Would you like to continue?"

Much to your chagrin, your youngster persists, and you continue to escalate the punishment. His rage is out of control, and the more you try to punish him to convince him to stop and calm down, the worse he becomes.

There is a term for this type of discipline: consequence stacking. The parent is losing emotional control in this situation. When your child is distressed, it is difficult to tolerate. It irritates us. However, you should ask yourself, "What do I want my child to learn?"

And the answer is likely something like, "I want him to learn not to cry every time he has to do something he doesn't want to do." or "I want him to understand that when he gets upset, there is a proper way to deal with it."

The worst thing you can do is join him in his anguish. Harsh penalties that appear to be never-ending to your child are ineffective and will just make him angry at the time. Remember, the idea is to teach your child self-control. Although effective and well-thought-out consequences are important, punitive consequence stacking is not the solution.

## Take a Rest

During coaching sessions, I frequently ask parents to reflect on their own disagreements. "When you and your spouse are irritated at one other, what do you do to calm down?" Frequently, they declare they will take a break and do something on their own for a brief period of time until they can calm down and speak things over.

This strategy also works with your child, but many parents do not consider it since they believe they should have control over their children. Keep in mind, however, that when someone is angry, you can't argue with them, and you can't rush things.

When you continue to engage one another in anger, the problem is not resolved. In fact, it often escalates. When you are in a disagreement with your child, take a break, then, when everyone has calmed down, come back together for an honest and open discussion.

Content related to: Child Outbursts: Why Do Children Blame, Make Excuses, and Fight When Their Behavior Is Challenged?

## Demonstrate Appropriate Reactions to Anger

I also advise parents to attempt to be role models for how to cope with anger responsibly. In other words, utilize your own anger management as a teaching tool for your child. What are some excellent approaches? When necessary, tell your youngster, "I'm feeling frustrated—I'm going to take a break," and leave the room. Another example is, "I can't talk to you right now. I'm pretty upset, so I'll wait till I'm calm. Let's talk about it afterwards."

Admitting that you're angry and need time to cool down is not a sign of weakness. To the contrary, it takes a lot of courage to speak these thoughts aloud. Remember, you're teaching your child how to handle his or her anger, and that's precisely what you want him or her to learn.

# Chapter 15:
# Strategies to Positive Parenting and Managing an Explosive Child

## Help Your Child but Set Limits

We always want to rescue our children when they're in a rush. Unfortunately, doing so repeatedly prevents them from developing the independence needed in adulthood. The more you do things for your children, the more they will rely on you and the less they'll do for themselves.

Be supportive, but let your child do specific tasks by himself. For instance, when it comes to homework, encourage him to work on it without your help. If you need to monitor your child, don't hover. Sit near him, and work on your own task. It is an excellent time to tackle unfinished reports, update your blog, and the like.

## Practice Patience

Patience is a quality that all parents require, but it is significant for parents of children with explosions. While it is natural for parents to solve their children's problems and cure their explosions, most children require time to develop. According to National Institute of Mental Health (NIMH) and other studies, children with explosive tendencies develop similarly to their peers, except for brain development, where they lag by about three years. According to these studies, parents may be confident that their children will eventually develop the necessary organizational, planning, and judgment skills demonstrated by children who do not have behavioral disorders. However, the slower maturation path may necessitate more patience and a focus on long-term development rather than quick fixes.

## Get Down to Their Level

What this means is that you need to look at the situation from your child's perspective. Just because you see things one way does not mean that your child sees them the same way.

For starters, you have more experience, simply by virtue of being older. This combined with the explosive disorders factor can make things hard to identify with if you simply compare their experiences to your own. Rather than focusing on comparisons, consider from where your child is coming. Doing so will help your child understand that you see and respect them foe who they are, which fosters trust.

## Create a Healthy Environment

The environment that you create in your home affects your child tremendously. You already know this, but it will become even more evident as your child grows up. Make sure the entire household is a healthy and stable place where your child knows they are safe. Any uncertainty or toxicity will negatively affect your child. Directly or subconsciously, these instances will affect their behavior and possibly trigger their explosive disorders symptoms.

You can create a healthier home environment by controlling who visits. If you know that certain people are not positive influences on your child, then you should not let them into your home. Although it sounds harsh, it is a simple solution that will save your child a lot of hassle as they grow up. You cannot punish your child for acting out if this is the behavior they see other people exhibit in your household.

If you find that someone who is already living under your roof is causing issues, you need to take that person aside to discuss how their behavior disrupts the environment. Ensure they do not feel attacked by explaining how everyone who is living under the same roof will benefit from behaving better.

These kinds of actions ensure that you are keeping an overall stable and loving household environment.

## Keep Things Positive

Even when you are shelling out the discipline, there is no need to approach things negatively. Your child already knows that they did something wrong and that they are being taught a lesson, and it can be done in a non-confrontational way. Using this approach will allow your child to see that they can treat others in the same manner.

Be mindful of your tone when you are teaching your child something that you want them to do or correcting their behavior—a lighthearted but firm tone makes a difference. Your instructions are already clear, so there is no reason to harp on your child for why they are not following them or why they messed up.

You know that their explosive disorder can be challenging to deal with. Instead, you should focus on the solution.

## Communicate with Teachers and Other Professionals

Communicate openly and honestly with your child's teachers and other adults who interact with them, such as camp counselors. Children with explosive disorders have a legal right to special school accommodations, such as an Individualized Education Program (IEP), to help them succeed. Many parents, however, try to conceal the diagnosis of a behavioral disorder for fear of stigmatizing their child.

Teachers and others in teaching and caregiving roles may assume a child is willfully defiant or disruptive if they are unaware of the diagnosis. If you communicate openly about your child's difficulties, teachers will be able to work with him or her more effectively. This is not an opportunity to ask that their children be excused from assignments. Instead, they should consult with teachers about how to assist their children in completing their schoolwork.

## Research More about Explosive Disorders

Parents need to understand their children's behavior to help them fight the battle. That's why there is a variety of support groups for parents who have children with explosive disorders. Aside from that, there's an influx of reliable sources on the Internet to help you figure out your child.

# Chapter 16:
# Show Respect to Get the Respect of an Explosive Child

The word "respect" is a personal term that means different things to different people. You respect your mom and dad, your children, and elderly family members. Respect is earned by certain behaviors and some people have more of that type of respect than others. But regardless of what you think it means, you will never earn respect without giving it in return, no matter the form. So why is it that some people are respected, while others aren't?

Is it because they've done more than the rest of us? Is it because they're more successful and have more material wealth than their peers? No. It's because they've proven themselves on the field of battle, in areas not related to material wealth. It's because they have shown their worth and earned the respect of others through tangible, measurable achievements.

Lack of respect leads to anger and then frustration, which may lead to explosive behaviors. Children need time to breathe and think and discover and play. They can't do all that children are supposed to do if you are hover over them, waiting for the next outburst.

Being with the child is enough. You don't need words of affirmation at all. Be with them and spend time with them and they will begin to accept that you are going to stay and that they are wanted. The greatest thing you could do is just be nearby, be quiet and connected.

It won't happen overnight, but it will happen if you show respect, give positive attention, and speak with the child in a manner that is appropriate for their age level.

Children need to feel wanted and needed, not alone and neglected. They become persistent if you ignore them and will test you in unusual ways. This is what's called "defensive pushing" and for a child, this is their way of finding out how much love they have inside themselves. It's also how they express their need for attention.

When a child is pushing you, it's just to show you that they are doing things. They are trying to gain your attention, and if you don't pay them the right kind of attention, they become frustrated and angry very quickly. The more frustration they have inside themselves, the more explosive behaviors they create.

To decrease these explosions, we need to make sure that we don't ignore our children when they attempt to contact us. We need to show patience and respect for the fact that they are children. When you interact with them, you don't have to say anything. It can be as simple as touching them or just saying a few words to let them know that you understand what they're saying.

The key is to be present for your child. It gives them a good sense of being wanted and needed, which is important for an explosive child. It helps them build up their self-esteem and self-worth at an early age.

When they think they are not good enough, they overreact to things because they feel vulnerable and weak. When a child doesn't feel good enough is when the explosive behaviors begin and when the child becomes extremely sensitive to any type of criticism.

Conversely, when a child feels like they have worth, they feel more confident, and they are less likely to overreact. They can do what they want to do because they don't have to worry about anyone judging them.

If you have an explosive child who is going through a phase, be available to them. Give them positive attention to help them through their anger, sadness, or frustration, and show them that they are good. With positive attention from you, they will see themselves in a more positive light, which also shows them that you are a stable, loving person. This will make them feel like they have something to look forward to in life and you can help them to figure out what it is that they want from life.

You can also take children out for adventure, as it will help to stabilize them and give them something to focus on. It provides a sense of freedom and gives them a break from all the pressure they've put upon themselves. They need independence, self-reliance, and knowledge of who they are as individual people. This will help them learn to respect people more because they can see that there are other things out there to do rather than look at the TV all day, eat junk food, or play video games. If you let your child explore, there is a good chance you will see a positive change in their behavior.

Parents should give children the responsibility of self-direction, motivation, and independence that allows children to take control over what happens in their lives. Children need to be allowed to discover what they want in life. They need to know how to make things happen and how to motivate themselves. This will help them learn about the world around them and how it relates to them.

Give them more opportunities to play with other children to learn how to better work together. They didn't want what you wanted for them so let them work it out for themselves. The problem with that is that if you can't solve the situation yourself and find a resolution with the other parents, you'll be out of a job. There are so many things that you can do to keep your children busy.

You can take your child to new places or teach them new things, such as playing a musical instrument or how to draw or paint. Perhaps your child is interested in how thing work and would enjoy a lesson in auto mechanics, electricity, or engineering. If you look at it positively enough, you'll be surprised at how much you have learned from it yourself.

# Chapter 17:
# Teach Them to Accept Constructive Criticism

When children don't give their best effort, they are often criticized by others. This criticism may lead to their feeling ashamed or embarrassed, which is not a good thing. Parents are tasked with teaching their children how to cope with constructive criticism in the right way.

Children need to learn that they have the right to decide what they will do and what they will not do. Parents should always respect their children and, within reason, do as they are asked. However, when children are not respectful towards their parents, they will likely not respect others when it is time for them to start making choices. Therefore, this lesson is critical.

Parents should make sure that they provide their children with some guidance in decision-making even if they are acting on their own. Children should be provided with options.

Parents should also assure that they are not putting too much pressure on their children to do well in school. Doing so may cause the child unnecessary frustration, leading to failure to perform to their ability. The greatest way for parents to teach their children how to accept constructive criticism is by showing them how they can deal with their own criticism in a positive manner.

These are the 8 best ways to teach your child about constructive criticism.

1. Make sure that they understand how they can determine their own values.

When children are young, they don't think about what is right and wrong or what to value and not value in life. Instead, their parents hold them accountable for their choices and ensure they understand how to make good decisions most of the time.

In doing so, you will first show them how they can be productive members of society by valuing the right things and finding ways to improve on their mistakes. For example, if you tell your child that he or she didn't clean his or her room, you should then ask them what they think it is important to do to be a good member of the family.

2. Make sure that they understand how to act in a respectful manner.

Parents should make sure that they are certain that their children are acting in a respectful manner toward people around them. This is usually something that many parents fail to realize, but it's important for your child to know early on. By making them aware of their behavior as well as providing them with tools for improvement, you will make sure that they don't grow up feeling ashamed or comfortable acting disrespectfully towards others. For example, if your child is being disrespectful to another person, you should tell them to apologize.

3. Set clear limits for your child.

It's extremely important for parents to set clear limits for their children so they understand what they can and cannot do. Parents should also need to make sure that they explain why these rules are in place and why it's important for them to act in certain ways. Most parents set rules and only give explanations when children are breaking the rules or asking questions about how things work. It is not a good idea because children will never learn how to understand the rules and avoid breaking them. Instead, parents should set clear limits on what their children can do, even when they don't understand why these rules are in place. For example, it's important for your child to know that he or she cannot hit other people without getting a consequence for it.

4. Make sure that they understand how to resolve conflicts in a healthy way.

Children need to be taught how to resolve conflict in a healthy way so that they can learn to work out differences and make decisions that benefit everyone involved. By allowing your child to be part of the solution, you will soon realize how they can show others how to resolve their own problems without feeling as though they are being unfairly treated or blamed for a mistake. For example, if your child has a disagreement with another child, you should make them aware of who they can ask for help if they are interested in solving the problem.

5. Help them to understand why people are behaving the way that they are.

It's important for children to understand why other people act in a certain manner when it comes to their friends, families, and classmates. This means that children need to be taught how to figure out exactly what other people mean and give them the tools that they need to do so. Your child needs to understand where they need to focus their attention and what they need to consider before deciding.

6. Help them understand how their actions affect others.

Children need to understand how their actions affect other people, even when they don't mean to be disrespectful or rude in any way. This means that children need to know that the people in their lives will be affected by things that are said, done, or witnessed. When you make your child aware of these things, you will soon realize how they will be able to show others that everyone around them matters and that treating other people poorly can have serious consequences for them.

7. Teach them why their mistakes are important.

When children learn about their mistakes, they understand how to avoid making similar mistakes in the future. This is a powerful lesson for children because it will give them control over their choices and decisions. Most children feel worse when they are criticized; instead of berating them, encourage them to discuss what happened and devise ways to prevent the same thing from happening again.

8. Let them know when they are doing something correctly.

Although most people know how to criticize others, very few people are good at showing praise when it is deserved. It's critical for parents to make sure that they praise their children when they do something well. It could be so hard for children to see the positive side of things when they are being told they've been bad because they end up feeling as though they aren't good enough. When you think about how you show your child gratitude, you should choose to praise them instead of criticizing them.

## Express Anger Positively

It's important for your child to develop the ability to express their anger without hurting others. Anger is a normal emotion, and it can be very difficult for children to learn what they need to do for it not to escalate into someone being injured. When there is a major disagreement between you and your child about how something should be handled, with them. You don't want them to believe they are incapable of thinking of ways that they could have changed things differently.

If parents express anger in an inappropriate manner, their children will often learn how to do the same. Parents can help their children address the way that they express their feelings in an unhealthy manner by setting boundaries for themselves. Ultimately, this will lead to better control over themselves and a healthier way of expressing themselves.

When you don't show your children how to process anger appropriately, then they are going to have a very difficult time in life. It's not something that you can teach them once and assume they learned. Instead, you need to continue working with your child throughout their life on how to handle anger and frustration. When the two of you are dealing with anger, you need to use everyday language. If your child is telling you that they are angry, then try and respond in a positive way. Sometimes it is helpful for them to tell others about their anger as well if it makes them feel better. It can be very confusing for them when they don't know what to say to someone who genuinely cares about their feelings.

Working towards developing a positive expression of their anger will make your child feel better about themselves because they understand what to say and how not to hurt another person. Even if your child isn't particularly good at expressing their feelings, you can work on this together once the basics are understood.

To properly express anger, a child must understand why they feel the way that they do. Parents can help their children by pointing out how they were feeling and what made them feel the way that they did. The parent should explain what he or she felt and what causes his or her feelings. Doing so allows children to better understand their own emotions and come to terms with them more easily. Parents must also educate their children on how to express their anger in a productive manner.

In addition, parents can teach their child how to properly deal with anger through constructive outlets such as sports, art, or other activities. Parents should also take the time to discuss what a child can do when they feel angry. These discussions will allow them to learn how to deal with situations that cause anger in a constructive manner. They may also be able to express themselves verbally by explaining their feelings and frustration over an inappropriate situation.

# Chapter 18:
# Your Marital Life Affects Your Child

Among the many responses given by a set of research respondents when challenged how they might tell whether a couple was married, one common answer was "if they are arguing, then they are married." Although this may be amusing, it may be teaching the children in the house the wrong lesson about dealing with frustrations. Their responses may be considerably more frightening and ought to be considered.

Even if we don't want them to, our children are always keeping an eye on us. When it comes to absorbing the emotional climate around them, children are like sponges. They are acutely aware of every frustrated eye roll and every muttered criticism directed at their parents' bond. Even though we attempt to hide our difficulties from our children, they are aware of them and are affected by how their parents interact.

Many of us can recall instances from our upbringings when our parents were so consumed by their feelings and emotions that they acted as if we were not in the room. It happens from time to time because we get so caught up in an engagement with our spouse that we forget that we have an audience.

We may attempt to trick ourselves into thinking that they are preoccupied with something; however, when it concerns the relationships between their parents, they will miss little. We all know someone who has a difficult connection with their child, and these behaviors affect our children while they are small. As they mature, they frequently re-enact the same tendencies in their interactions, which is not healthy for anybody.

A child's anxiety and concern about the future generally rises when they suspect anything is amiss with their parents. They may begin to hurt themselves to distance themselves from their feelings. If they are fearful, depressed, or insecure, they may attempt to numb their feelings by engaging in habits such as excessive eating or obsessive video gaming. Whenever children don't feel they can express themselves verbally to their parents, or when their frustration or hurt encompasses their parents, they may begin to show their emotions unintentionally, such as by having a meltdown over toys, becoming abnormally needy towards another parent, having lost interest in education, or picking fights with other youngsters.

Whatever a child's preferred method of releasing his or her feelings, one emotion that tends to affect every youngster whose family is experiencing difficulties is guilt. It is quite common for children to bear the responsibility and feel under pressure to set things right in their home when their parents are having difficulties. hat this wouldn't have occurred if they'd been better is a common notion for children. Unfortunately, small children are often neglected on an emotional level at a moment when they require the most support to make sense of the emotions they feel with the upheaval in the home. As a result of this strain, even if children are less developed than their parents, they become melancholy and agitated because of having to cater to the needs and desires of everyone. It's common for parents who are fighting with one another to ask their children to pick sides, thus pulling the child into the heart of the quarrel and giving them a role with which they are ill-equipped to deal.

If a parent feels bad about their actions or a relationship, for example, he or she may not be aware of how much stress it is placing on the child, but other times the strains that parents put on their children may be more subtle. When parents are unable to satisfy one other's emotional needs, they commonly turn to their children for assistance. This lays an unnatural and damaging load on a youngster, even though it is frequently unconsciously done. It has been shown that when parents are satisfied and pleased with themselves and their relationships in general, they become less capable of exerting influence upon their children. When parents' own mental needs are addressed, they can provide their children with a feeling of peace and stability from which to explore the world around them. Children may feel joyful because their parents are happy, and they can trust that their parents will supply their needs and desires.

## How Disagreements Between Parents Have a Genuine Impact on their Children

Parental conflicts are typical, yet the method by which these arguments affect children varies significantly. What could parents do to reduce the damage that their disagreements cause? What occurs at home has a significant effect on the overall cognitive growth and wellbeing of children. Although the connection between a parent and child is vital, it is not the only one.

A child's well-being is also influenced by how their parents interact with one other, which may impact everything from their mental health to their academic performance and their future relationships. However, there is the possibility that something nice may emerge out of a "wonderful" row. For the most part, disputes don't harm children. It is possible, however, for difficulties to occur when parents argue and get engaged with one another when they constantly retreat or start giving one another "cold shoulder." Exposing children to tension may well have elevated heart rates and stress hormone reactions as early as the six-months of age, according to the UK and worldwide research was undertaken over many years via surveillance in the household, lengthy follow-up work, and field experiments.

When there is an extreme amount of tension between the parents, children and adolescents are more likely to suffer from sleep deprivation, stress, despair, and other mental health issues. Exposure of children is continuing, but the less extreme conflict has similar impacts when contrasted to students whose families discuss or productively settle issues.

Which Is More Important, Nature or Nurture?

The consequences for children are not always as obvious as one would assume. Consider the case of divorce, which is frequently viewed as having an extremely severe and long-lasting impact on many youngsters, as well as the decision by parents to separate.

However, it is now believed that in some situations, rather than the break-up itself, it is the fights that occur among parents beforehand, throughout, and then after the breakup that do the most harm.

A similar assumption has been made about how children react to disagreement in the past: that their genetics have a role in their response.

Ultimately, nature has a key role in children's mental health, including stress, anxiety, and mental illness. However, their home setting, as well as the nurturing they receive there, might be quite important. It is becoming more recognized that inherited biological concerns for mental health issues may be worsened - or altered - by one's family's experiences.

What matters most is to how well you and your partner are getting along, whether you're living together or not, and not whether the children are biologically related, or you've adopted them.

## Arguments About Children

What does this imply for parents, and how should they respond? First, it is critical to acknowledge that it is natural for parents and caregivers to disagree or quarrel with one another. Children, on the other hand, fair worse when their parents engage in frequent, heated, and unresolved confrontations with one other.

And this is especially true if the dispute involves children, such as when youngsters blame themselves or believe they are to blame for the conflicts. Children and adolescents who experience negative consequences may experience sleep disturbances and interrupted neurodevelopment in infancy, anxiety and behavioral problems in preschool, anxiety, and academic difficulties, as well as other severe problems such as self-harm, in teenagers. It has been well documented for many years that household abuse and exploitation may have especially negative consequences on children who are involved. However, parents don't need to engage in volatile or hostile behavior against one another for harm to be done.

It is also detrimental to children's emotional, behavioral, and social development when they grow reclusive or display low levels of warmth towards one another. Unfortunately, the difficulties do not stop there. The effects of dysfunctional relationships on children are not just seen by them in their own lives; study has shown that they may be passed down from one generation to another. The cycle must be interrupted if we are to ensure that today's generation of children, and maybe the next generation of families will enjoy good and happy lives.

## Having a "Personal" Argument

According to a study, children are keen monitors of their parent's conduct from the age of approximately two—and maybe from an even earlier age. It is common for them to notice disputes, even when parents feel their children are not aware of them or assume they have shielded them by fighting privately.

In the end, it is how children perceive and comprehend the reasons and possible repercussions of disputes that are important to consider. Children make decisions about whether they believe disputes are likely to grow, whether they believe they will be involved, and if they believe they will represent a threat to social stability—a worry that is particularly relevant for small children.

They may also be concerned about the chance that their connection with their parents will deteriorate as a consequence. Girls are more prone to emotional issues and boys are more prone to behavioral issues, according to a study.

In many cases, strategies aiming at promoting the mental health of children and adolescents have focused on assisting the children directly and supporting their parents. While supporting the bond between parents may make a significant impact on children in the near term, it is also possible that encouraging the relationship between parents may best prepare them to develop positive interactions with others in the coming years. Fostering the healthy development of children requires the presence of positive interactions with family members, relatives, other grownups (e.g., educators), and companions in the early years of a child's life. What occurs at home may have a significant impact on these connections, whether for the better or the worse.

For parents who are worried about the influence their disagreements could have on their children, it is only reasonable to be worried. However, it is common for parents to quarrel or argue with their children from time to time, and children react positively when their parents clarify or settle a disagreement adequately. Indeed, when parents can effectively settle disagreements, their children may acquire valuable skills that will help them manage their personal emotional experiences outside of the family circle in the future. Giving parents the capacity to comprehend how their interactions with their children impact their children's development lays the groundwork for healthy children now—and for stable families in the long term.

# Chapter 19:
# Help Children Express Themselves

Because of their social immaturity, small children are unable to express themselves in a healthy manner. However, as they develop language skills and command an ever-growing vocabulary, temper-tantrums should cease for the most part. When they don't, however, the inability to communicate effectively often leads to emotional problems. The child will need guidance and support to learn to appropriately express their emotions in a productive manner. To learn how to express themselves, they will need the support of their parents and the help of their teachers.

Directive parenting is a style of parenting that focuses on creating order by giving orders rather than letting children make reasonable decisions for themselves. Parents who use this style often view their children as extensions of themselves. In such a case, the child will not be able to express themselves in a productive manner. Those children are often caught between their parents and peers, and they are left unable to separate themselves from their parents or their peers.

Parents who model aggressive and manipulative behavior by displaying extreme behaviors to control and manipulate their children may cause confusion for the children. Such children may resort to destructive behaviors to manipulate their parents. In turn, parents need to be aware of their own behavior and the way it affects their children, and they should set limits for themselves.

Parents also must allow their children to express themselves in a healthy manner by giving them the opportunity to talk about their feelings to understand them. In addition, parents need to be involved with any school system that allows its students room for self-expression. This will give them an outlet for their feelings in a productive manner. Parents should encourage their children to join activities that allow them to express themselves through artistic means, such as music or dance.

Children who are allowed to take part in activities that allow them to develop their creativity and self-expression will be able to better resolve conflicts among others that they may face in the future. In addition, they will be able to separate themselves from their parents and peers in a healthy manner, which is crucial to emotional development.

Parents should also encourage their children to explore and learn about new things. Children who express themselves will be able to make the right choices in life, and they will be more successful when they make the right choices.

Children need to interact with others by playing with them, graduating from one activity or game to another, or going for a walk. Parents should not expect that their explosive child can handle more than one activity at a time because it is often too difficult for them. Understanding their needs gives them the opportunity to understand how to express themselves. Parents should also allow their children to be independent and make their own decisions about trivial things to help them build he confidence they will need in the future to make significant decisions.

A sense of self-worth is crucial for a child to make good decisions. By allowing them to do something on their own, they express themselves positively and have a good feeling of accomplishment when they complete a task on their own.

Parents can encourage their children by supporting them in whatever it is that they wish to pursue in life. When a child wants to play a certain sport or become a doctor, parents will have to support them. Children will gain confidence when they are able to express themselves, and they will learn that the world is full of different people who want to help them. By helping their children develop this sense of confidence and self-esteem, they find fulfillment in their lives.

## Help them deal with change

Children should have the opportunity to cope with change by trying new things as they get older. Begin with insignificant things and help them build to more critical decisions that have lasting consequences. In strategically ramping up the complexity of the decision-making process, the child will have the chance to understand the ramifications of the decisions they make. Success builds confidence while failures offer learning opportunities. They can survive and manage their feelings about changes by trying new things in their life, which will teach them how to cope with change. They can also make the right choices by deciding based on their own personal interests rather than being pressured by others.

Parents often want their children to respond to change by taking defensive measures, which comes from fear of the unknown rather than understanding it. This is a loss of self-esteem that happens when a child is forced to conform or behave in an abnormal manner just because he or she does not understand something.

Children are often forced to adapt to change. Parents should help them to do so by allowing their children the option of maintaining their personality, beliefs, and hobbies the way he or she wants it to be. They will also want to educate their children at an early age about how changing attitudes and demands in adolescence can affect one's life. The child should be able to adjust to change by becoming more independent and dealing with it successfully.

The most crucial thing that parents can do is teach their children how to cope with change by helping them understand that they are not alone. Children should be taught how to deal with change by making good choices. They should gain the knowledge and experience needed to cope with change and express themselves.

## Help them deal with peer pressure

Peer pressure is a result of faulty socialization, and it is a cause of many emotional problems. Children who are under too much pressure from their peers can become overly dependent on the approval of others because they are unable to express themselves to cope with their emotions. They start to place themselves in situations that are inappropriate for them based on the favoritism of others.

Parents must try to prevent their children from becoming dependent on the opinions of others. They should also encourage their children by showing them how to make good choices, no matter what anyone else says. These are important lessons that they need to learn for their child to be able to make good choices when they grow up.

For children to avoid being placed in situations that are inappropriate for them, parents should encourage their children by making good choices, which they need to learn how to do before the social pressure evolves as children age. They should also make sure that there is open communication between the parent and the child. This way, the child will be secure in the support of a parent if someone is pressuring them else.

Parents must also provide their children the opportunity to make good choices by standing up for themselves. They should not allow anyone to put their child in a situation that is inappropriate for them or pressure them into doing something they don't want to do or know they shouldn't do. They should know how to deal with peer pressure, which will help them understand how to make good choices at an early age.

## Help them build good relationships

Parents must devote time to educate their children how to make good relationships because relationships are important in life. When children understand this, they will not be afraid of making friendships or being seen with others. They will also realize that there are many benefits that come from having good relationships with others.

Parents must spend quality time with their children to teach them about how important it is for them to have great relationships. When children spend quality time with their parents, they learn about relationships through positive role models. Parents must allow their children have a say in whatever it is that they want to do and make sure that their children understand how to respect others.

An additional positive to spending time with their children is that the parents cultivate a lasting and positive relationship with their children. Children need to be taught to respect others and the importance of good behavior because this will help them have good relationships when they get older. Parents need to be supportive of their children for them to develop healthy relationships.

## Help them develop a consistent lifestyle

It's important for your child to develop a consistent lifestyle and know what to expect from the day. Your child should always know what their responsibilities are, and you should work with them on this. If you don't establish a routine at an early age, then it will be difficult for them when they get to school. Many children live in fear that they won't be able to do something that is expected of them if they have no idea what will happen next or how to handle it successfully.

Your child needs to know that life will be challenging, and that they need to be able to deal with the results of their actions. You do want your child to develop a routine, but you want it to be flexible enough that it can be adjusted during the week. If your child has constant routines, then they are going to get in trouble when things don't go according to plan.

You shouldn't give your child every little detail about their schedule because then they won't have any reason to develop independence. It's better for them if you let them know what time you are leaving for work and let them decide how they are going to spend their day. They need to know that they are going to have to make decisions and figure out how to handle them.

They need to know what they could expect, and they should be able to handle things at school and at home. If your child is developmentally ready to learn how to manage their responsibilities, then they will do better in life. You are setting them up for a success by giving them a plan that they can understand and follow.

If you are struggling with a low self-esteem child, then encourage them to develop a routine and set goals that they should be able to achieve. When this is done, then you can start to take more of a hands-off approach in their lives.

Your child needs to do what they are told, yet it's important for them to have control over some aspects of their lives. Even if you don't think that you are effective or know what is best for them, your child will feel better about themselves when they know that you care about them and let them make decisions.

Give your child a goal and give him or her the steps that they need to take to achieve their goal. Your child needs to develop a plan; from there, they need to be able to determine the steps necessary to finish successfully. Then, they need to schedule their time so that they can accomplish everything. If they run into a roadblock, they will have the means to determine the best way to still achieve that goal. Thus, they are motivated and prepared for the fact that they may have to change their plan. This will give them the motivation that they need to get started.

This is much better than telling them what needs done and then getting frustrated because they didn't do it correctly. When you are constantly telling your child what you want from them, it can be very demotivating for them. You are essentially telling them that you don't believe they are ready for this type of responsibility, even if they think they are. Your child needs to feel like they know what you want and that they are capable. This will give them confidence in themselves.

## Help them develop good habits

A good habit is one that is done often and results in good behavior. Having a bad habit is doing the same action repeatedly—usually without any result. A habit can be something you do every day when you get up in the morning or something that only happens once a week. The more you do it, the more likely it will become a habit.

Developing good habits is one way to help your child handle anger management problems. Your child's age will affect which habits are most helpful for them to develop; however, the most important habits your child can develop are those that will help them learn calming and positive ways to handle the feelings of anger and frustration.

There are several habits that are easy to set up to help a child get better at managing anger. Each of these habits should be practiced every day until they are habits. It may take some time for them to stick, but with your help, your child can learn how to calm down and relax when he or she is angry. These habits will help them become more independent and less dependent on you for their sense of safety.

1. **Positive thinking:** Positive thinking is the belief that things will turn out well in life. Maintaining a positive outlook will help a child focus when anger threatens to consume them.
2. **Stop and take a break:** Teach your child is to stop what they are doing when they get angry and take a break from whatever caused the anger in the first place. When children misbehave, it often happens because of something you said or did that caused frustration and removing oneself from the situation helps them from becoming more frustrated.

3. **Don't bring home your bad mood:** Another good habit is to avoid bringing a bad mood home. Children can sometimes become more frustrated when they are waiting for you, which may make them angrier. Leaving your bad day outside will help them feel better and keep them from getting further frustrated.
4. **No self-expression until you have calmed down:** Ask children not to express themselves emotionally until they have calmed down and their anger has subsided. A child's anger often signals that he or she needs help, but frequently children will use their anger to try and solve problems without asking for help. When children are calm, it helps them focus on solving the problem and may make it easier for them to ask for help.
5. **Don't say anything you will regret later:** When a child is angry, don't say anything you will regret later as the child incorrectly interpret what their parents are saying, which leads to more anger. Stop before you say anything that will make your child feel worse about himself or herself—or about you.
6. **Respect**: The best habit a child can learn is to respect himself and others. Children who learn to respect themselves are more willing to listen and accept constructive guidance from their parents. When they respect themselves, they are better able to listen to reason and learn how to solve problems without becoming angry or resorting to outbursts.
7. **Seek help:** When a child is upset, he or she needs help solving the problem, not more frustration from you or someone else. Children who are kept close for too long often get more frustrated because of isolation—and this will make them angry at you as well as at the situation itself.
8. **Teach them new ways of self-protection:** Finally, teach children new ways to handle their anger. Some children may need to learn how to step back and calm themselves when they get angry so they can continue with what they were doing and not get even more frustrated. Some children may need to learn how to control the anger, so it doesn't cause physical harm.

Whenever a child gets angry, it is important not only for them but also for the adults in their lives that they continue learning better habits of dealing with anger management problems. It may take some time, but these habits will help your child become less aggressive and more independent when he or she feels upset or angry.

# Chapter 20:
# Strategies to Disciplining Explosive Children

The fact that children who are reared with clear limits and direction are more likely to be happy, pleasant people with good self-control is one of the many essential reasons why you should discipline your children. Conversely, children who have been indulged with no limits or penalties are generally greedy, unable to self-regulate, and unpleasant to be around.

The solution: Set clear and consistent rules, boundaries, and consequences for your child. Keep the broader picture in mind if you're scared that disciplining your child may make them upset. A child's future will suffer if they are not disciplined. If you're in charge of them, give them good penalties with love and respect.

## Positive Discipline

Positive discipline is worth a try if you are uncomfortable spanking your child. Without resorting to threats, incentives, scolding, or physical punishment, you can often nip undesirable behavior in the bud by utilizing positive disciplinary strategies like redirection, praise, and selective ignoring. This disciplining strategy, according to proponents, can help develop ties and increase trust between parents and children. When you respond to provocation with these five tried-and-true examples of constructive discipline instead of anger, you're also teaching a youngster that it's possible to deal with difficult situations without getting into a fight.

## Redirection

An exceptional method for diffusing defiance and conflict rapidly is called redirection. When you redirect your child's focus, you are essentially breaking their attention away from one thing and guiding it toward something more positive. Turning their attention away from a trigger and toward a solution is an excellent example of redirection, though it can be achieved in many other ways, too.

Little ones have a short attention span, so redirecting them to another activity when they're acting out isn't difficult. Introduce another item that will capture your toddler's attention if he or she is playing with a potentially unsafe object. If that doesn't work, take them to a different room or outside to distract them.

Instead of telling an older child what they can't do, tell them what they can do. For example, rather than telling your youngster that they can no longer watch YouTube, tell them that they may go outdoors and play or work on a new puzzle. Focusing on the good can help you avoid a lot of fights and stubborn behavior.

If your child tends to habitually respond to certain triggers overwhelmingly, now is an excellent opportunity to practice redirecting their attention before the explosive outburst, which should result in a peaceful outcome. Learning to correctly perform this redirect will affect your child's habitual response into a more productive process, effectively diffusing any conflict before it arises.

For example, let's say putting your child's shoes on so you can leave the house is a common point of conflict, and every time you ask them to put their shoes on, they are triggered. You may notice that you tend to state the need to put their shoes on as follows: "Can you please put your shoes on so we can go grocery shopping?" At this point, you have already lost your child's attention at the point of asking them to put their shoes on, and they have begun melting down before you even finished your sentence.

Instead, you might say, "We need to go buy some more of your favorite snacks so you can have them to eat for school! Put your shoes on so we can go. [Hand them their shoes.] What flavor will you pick this time?" Following the second example, you emphasize focusing on the benefit they are getting from going out and minimizing the stress of putting their shoes on.

You can perform this sort of redirection in absolutely any situation, regardless of the subject of that situation. For it to be productive, though, you need to know what your child does not want to do, and what they do want to do. Structure your delivery by selling them on the benefit of getting to do what they want to do before asking them about what they tend to be triggered by. In turn, you maintain their positive attention, and they are more likely to comply.

## Discourage Yelling in the Home

While yelling across the house may seem like an easier way to get your child's attention than walking over to their room and talking to them, this can foster an increasingly stressful environment. Yelling through the door or wall at your child, or allowing them to yell at you this way, can set the tone for meltdowns rather quickly. During the yelling process, everyone is already elevating their energy through the simple act of shouting. Further, miscommunications are far more likely under these circumstances, and that can make for even larger meltdowns if you are not careful.

Instead, set a rule that everyone must speak within close enough proximity that you can converse with a calm voice. This means no more yelling across the house. Walk to where the other is before you start talking to each other. This way, yelling is discouraged, and peaceful, respectful communication is encouraged instead.

## Connection before Correction

Taking the time to connect with your child by hugging them and affirming that you love them before you begin correcting their behavior ensures that they first receive the support they require to navigate their troubling emotions. You can then discuss what was wrong with their behavior and educate them on a more positive means for dealing with their emotions in the future.

## Set Limits in a Loving Way

Punishment is typically used as a means of setting limits, though it is often negative or critical. Learning to set limits affectionately allows you to acknowledge and correct negative behavior without exploding into rages of anger or otherwise experiencing an undesirably emotional outburst with your child. For instance, let's imagine that your child wants to keep playing their game instead of getting ready for bed, so they become frustrated, and an outburst is imminent. Rather than retorting with "Too bad" or "It's time for bed, so stop playing, NOW!" you might try something along the lines of: "Wow you're enjoying this game aren't you! I understand it's hard to stop playing and get ready for bed. Let's continue with this game tomorrow." This way, you are acknowledging your child's feelings, having empathy for them, and still upholding the limits so you can encourage your child to do as they have been asked.

## Teach Your Child to Fix Their Mistakes

Making mistakes is an inevitable part of life, but children may be more prone to them, considering they have not learned from many of their own mistakes in the past. Further, they have not had the opportunity to properly learn how to adapt and navigate their mistakes, either. Teaching your child how to address and remedy their mistakes ensures they recognize how to overcome any potential adversities, and in turn, are more likely to navigate them peacefully.

When it comes to teaching your child how to navigate mistakes, always do so in a matter-of-fact way. Do not make a big deal about the mistake, as doing so may trigger an unnecessary emotional response, which makes dealing with the mistake far more challenging. Instead, acknowledge that a mistake happened and focus on fixing the mistake with your child, so they realize mistakes are not worth a major emotional outcry, and that they can easily be resolved and worked out.

## Time-In

Time-out can be an effective punishment, but it can be difficult to execute properly. According to research, 85 percent of parents who try to use this disciplinary technique fail. They wither talk with children or allow them to play with toys during time-outs. (Time-outs should be solitary and boring to be most effective.) If your instinct is to interact with your child rather than banish them, you might try a time-in. Rather than putting your child to time-out alone after a period of bad conduct, sit down with them and read a book together.

Time-ins are useful in and of themselves for promoting good conduct, but they are most successful when combined with well-executed time-outs regularly.

# Chapter 21:
# Behavioral Therapy for Explosive Children

Often abbreviated to CBT, cognitive-behavioral therapy is perfect for parents wishing to be actively involved with and active in their child's clinical development. CBT's focus is to train parents and other caregivers in the management of children's explosive symptoms.

One of the characteristics of being the parent of an explosive child is that it raises many doubts, irrational thoughts, and unrealistic expectations. While other therapies focus on direct actions, CBT helps you eliminate the roadblocks that prevent you from helping your child overcome his symptoms of explosivity.

Cognitive-behavioral therapy is one of the most effective types of psychotherapy. It aims to help a child change their behavior by managing daily reactions and actions. It usually involves practical assistance that seeks to establish tasks, complete schoolwork, and manage emotionally tricky situations. Behavioral therapy also instructs children to self-regulate. That enables a child to praise themself or reward themself for acting appropriately. By doing this, a child thinks before acting and avoids rash decisions. Additionally, parents and teachers can give the child positive or negative feedback for certain actions. Delineated and structured chores, lists, and rules may facilitate this process.

Well-implemented cognitive behavioral therapy will not only strive to change behaviors, but it will also seek to transform the very thinking processes that birth these behaviors. In short, cognitive-behavioral therapy is a unique approach to treating an explosive disorder naturally and sustainably. It allows children to evaluate how they feel. Why do they act the way they do? Why does one stimulus make them feel bad when another does not? How do classmates and teachers affect their moods? What do they think to themselves when negative feelings arise? How about when positive feelings occur? Ultimately, what can they do to ensure that when things go badly, they don't go that badly?

Therapists can also teach children social skills, including how to wait their turn, request help, share personal property, and respond appropriately to criticism. Children can even learn how to read body language, such as facial expressions and voice tone. That will enable them to understand more clearly social nuances and to act more appropriately for their age.

This therapy focuses on how behavior is affected by thoughts. Parents and therapists agree on the number of sessions a child needs before they are ready to adapt their behavior without constant sessions.

What does this form of therapy help the child with?

- It controls impulsivity and helps children develop self-control.
- Works on defiance and aggression and provides a coping mechanism and effective problem-solving skills.
- Helps with self-esteem issues and thus improves self-image issues.

## The Cognitive Behavior Therapy Technique

This type of therapy can be conducted in ways that include:

Parent-Child Sessions

These are common for a couple of reasons:

- To reconcile what the child told the therapist regarding their behavior to determine if they were being truthful without making the child feel as though they were doubting his words.
- To keep the parent updated on the progress of the child.
- To provide a platform for the child and the parent to have an open heart to heart conversation.
- To study the relationship between the child and the parent and the effect it has on the child.
- The parent is educated on parenting skills and how they affect the child.

Family-Based Sessions

These sessions involve more than just the parents. The siblings, close friends, and family members are invited into these sessions. Here, a couple of things happen. The therapist:

- Is privy to others' points of view on the condition.
- Understands how the condition affects them as individuals and their relationship with the child.
- Educates the extended family on an explosive disorder and sensitized over it.
- May invite the teachers to see how they interact and advise them on the best way to go about things at school.

Group Sessions

These sessions involve the child, the therapist, and other children dealing with the same condition. Sometimes parents are allowed to attend these sessions, and other times it is just the therapist and the children discussing a behavioral disorder and the challenges they face in their daily lives, as well as how they deal with it all. This type of interaction helps children realize that they are not alone in their experiences and that they are free to discuss their concerns without fear of being judged by others.

## Why Behavioral Therapy?

There are a few critical reasons why behavioral therapy should always be a part of explosive disorder treatment. To begin with, teens diagnosed with this disorder face daily problems that go well beyond their symptoms. Their inattentiveness, hyperactivity, and their impulsiveness only present one set of issues. There are additional problems that can appear as poor academic performance, misbehaving in school, or poor peer, sibling, and parental relationships. Your teen may disobey orders issued by adults and have other discipline problems.

Because they are predictors of how well your child will do overall, these problems are potentially serious, and you should not ignore them. Research indicates that how successful a child with the explosive disorder will be as an adult is best predicted by three factors:

1. The effectiveness of parenting skills
2. How well the child relates to other children
3. How well the child performs academically

There is no question that behavioral therapy effectively treats each of these domains. It instructs parents and teachers in methods that help them deal with an ADHD child. In the case of adolescents, it instructs them in helpful techniques for managing themselves. Once acquired, these skills can help the teen overcome their impairments. Because an explosive disorder is a chronic one, learning these skills is especially important. They will help a person diagnose it throughout their entire life.

Medication: The other component to treatment is medication. Unfortunately, there is a myth that medication loses its effectiveness over time. There is no evidence to support this. However, with the hormonal changes that begin with puberty, a child's receptivity to a particular drug might change. As part of the diagnosis of your teen, a new evaluation of the medication should take place. Your child's maturation may mean they need to be switched to a different drug therapy, or it may simply mean the dosage of their current drug should be increased.

Forms of Behavioral Therapy

Cognitive Behavioral Therapy, (CBT), is a therapeutic intervention that focuses on changing cognitive behaviors, improving emotional regulation, and developing coping strategies. Its focus is on behavior and helps children with explosive disorders learn organization skills, impulse control, and better way to manage their emotions.

## Behavioral Therapy Techniques

When your child is diagnosed with an explosive disorder, behavioral therapy is usually necessary. You still need to know what you should do to help your child when they are not in therapy by how you can improve their daily experience with helpful tips and tricks that many parents have been using for decades. These techniques are meant to give you a better understanding of how your child is feeling and what you can do to make their daily experiences less triggering. You will learn to recognize when your child is struggling because they will begin to act out or become hyperactive. These strategies will help you feel that you have more control of the situation. You can help your child and allow them to thrive in any environment.

There are certain fundamentals of behavioral therapy for behavioral disorders in children, and they are easy to understand. Even without a medical professional by your side, you as a parent can do so much to help your child. Most of the time, it involves getting them out of the situation they are in that is causing them distress. What you must remember is that your child is not neurotypical. This means that situations that may seem mundane to you or other children might seem entirely different to your child—and acceptance of this is the key.

These techniques can be used at any point by any parent. No matter how long your child has had their diagnosis, you can use these to assist you with difficult moments that usually seem impossible to get through. The thing about an explosive disorder is that it is fleeting. It reaches a peak, and then it simmers down if you know how to provide your child with the right coping skills. This is exactly what these techniques are designed for.

Make Sure Your Child Understands the Rules

Many parents lose their patience easily because they are often blind to the fact that a behavioral disorder prohibits children from being able to comprehend rules as easily as other children. Even if you have enforced them loud and clear, your child might still not understand what you expect from them. You need to be certain that they understand the rules, and there are several ways for you to do this without having to punish them over and over. Telling your child what to avoid or giving subtle hints is not going to work.

Give Clear Commands

After you know that you have their attention, you can give them the command exactly as you want it performed. Do not leave anything up for interpretation because your child's brain cannot handle vague information. For example, if you want them to take out the trash, tell them to take out the trash and put it in the bin outside. Then, you should tell them to replace the trash bag. This will avoid confusion and half-completed tasks. You need to give clear directions in this way so that they can truly comprehend what you expect from them. This is simply how your child's brain works, and there is nothing wrong with being direct.

Do Not Expect Perfection

There is no such thing as being perfect. Just as you will never be a perfect parent, there is never a moment when your child is going to behave perfectly. Perfection is a societal trap that makes you think you are not good enough and that you are not teaching your child enough. Instead of striving for perfection, recognize the circumstances. Notice when your child is doing the best that they can—given their circumstances. You must also recognize that you are doing the best you possibly can as a parent. This is good enough and should make you feel proud and accomplished. Perfection is subjective because there are many ways one can define the term. You might see perfection one way while someone else in your life sees it completely differently. Do not worry about reaching that state of ultimate perfection.

Adjust Your Rules as Your Child Gets Older

Your child is inevitably going to grow up quickly before your eyes. This means that you are going to have to make plenty of adjustments along the way, both with your parenting skills and the way that you discipline your child. The marble rewards system might become outdated as your child grows up, but you can still implement the same system verbally. Without focusing so much on points, you can simply state the consequences of their unruly behavior as they relate to the fun activities your child wants to do. No matter how old your child becomes, you are still going to be disciplining them as they live under your roof.

## **Strategies of Cognitive-Behavioral Therapy**

Determine the Condition

The therapist will first ask you or the child to define the problem, the symptoms, and whether they could be caused by something other than the condition. They will inquire about your children's interactions with others at school, at home, and elsewhere. They will inquire as to how the child's condition affects their relationship with their peers.

Examine Thoughts, Behaviors, and Emotions That Are a Result of the Condition

They will review the symptoms in detail and how they affect the child's thoughts, behavior, and emotions. The therapist will examine how the child reacts when their condition reveals the severity of the symptoms. How do they affect emotions in turn, and how long do the episodes last?

Spot the Negative Thoughts, Behavior, and Emotions Brought about by the Condition

The child will be asked how they deal with all this when it happens. Do they choose to hide from others, or do they own up to the result of their actions? The parent is then asked to support the claim.

Work to Replace the Dark Thought, Behavior, and Emotions Brought about by the Condition

When the symptoms become too severe, the therapist and the child come up with alternatives to replace the reaction to the emotions they feel. They talk about what to do if they become aggressive. They are taught coping mechanisms as well as how to perceive situations. The therapist collaborates with the child and parent to develop solutions and alternatives.

# Chapter 22:
# Multi-Modal Treatment

We know that three types of treatment can help ADHD patients: medication, behavior modification, and a combination of the two. Multi-modal treatment for ADHD patients entails using various strategies and techniques to manage the disease's symptoms.

Using a variety of treatments on children improves their chances of overcoming the condition. Many types of behavioral therapy do not require medication. You can suggest these behavior modification treatments to your doctor, who will be able to tell you which ones are best for your child. Many psychiatrists have used and researched these treatments.

## Behavioral Modification

For the past three decades, therapists have used Behavior Modification treatments to manage ADHD. Because of their experience and ability to cure many children of aggressive and disruptive behavior, these techniques have gained a lot of respect over the years. With the assistance of these methods, children with ADHD have learned to manage their actions, develop positive social skills, and improve their academic performance. There are five types of behavior modification treatments for children with ADHD:

- Cognitive Behavioral Interventions
- Clinical Behavior Therapy
- Direct Contingency Management
- Intensive Behavioral Treatments
- Behavioral and Pharmacological Treatment Combination

## Cognitive Behavior Therapy

This type of treatment, often abbreviated to CBT, is ideal for parents who want to be involved and active in their child's clinical development. CBT aims to teach parents and other caregivers how to manage their children's ADHD symptoms. It typically consists of training programs or individual sessions in which a therapist discusses how you can modify your child's behavior.

One of the characteristics of having an ADHD child is that it causes many doubts, irrational thoughts, and unrealistic expectations. While other therapies focus on direct actions, CBT assists you in removing the barriers that prevent you from helping your child in overcoming his ADHD symptoms. When it comes to ADHD and their child, many of the parents I speak with admit the following habits when assessing their child's development:

- Exaggeration: These parents believe that a single negative aspect of ADHD is more significant than all others. As a result, they may overlook significant broader progress.
- It's All or Nothing: If it doesn't work correctly, it doesn't work at all! Parents must recognize that each milestone achieved is perfect in its own right. When it comes to ADHD treatment, there is no such thing as "all or nothing." Patience pays off.
- "Should" Thinking: This type of thought process causes self-resentment when you fail to do something you believe you should do. However, there are no "shoulds." Just keep doing what the professional has asked or advised you to do, and don't add to your stress by constantly researching what else you could do to help your child.
- Comparative Thinking: This can be harmful to the mind. When you find yourself negatively comparing yourself to other parents of ADHD children, remember that each ADHD case is unique.
- Personalization: You are emotionally invested in your child's illness. You can ask yourself, "What did I do to deserve this?" or you can decide, "This is karma at work." It's not your fault that you have a difficult life, or your child has ADHD (unless you did not take care of yourself during pregnancy). As a result, don't take things personally.

Once you recognize such thoughts as disabling, you can confidently eliminate them and focus on the plan with the help of CBT. You must understand that you must first change your thoughts to make a significant difference in your child's life and mind.

## Cognitive Behavioral Interventions

This method is commonly referred to as CBI. The goal of CBI is to focus on self-control through verbal self-instruction and problem-solving strategies, self-monitoring and evaluation, cognitive modeling, and other similar techniques. Your child will meet with a therapist once or twice a week to learn these strategies through methods such as role-play.

Therapists use a popular CBI technique that teaches a child to "stop" when he is disruptive. These self-instruction techniques have been introduced when children with ADHD do not have the motivation to give themselves cues on what to do. Cognitive-behavioral interventions are becoming less popular as ADHD experts focus on developing alternative techniques.

## Contingency Management

This type of behavioral treatment, known as CM, follows a structured format and may include a special treatment classroom. The encouragement of actions through positive or negative reinforcement is one of the main principles used in CM. It entails using economic tokens as behavioral tools, such as the giving or withholding of rewards. Though most parents are accustomed to using reward systems with their children, knowing the most effective methods of achieving results can be beneficial. After receiving CM treatment, your child will be better able to respond to your cues as well as the prohibitions and privileges you grant him.

## Intensive Behavioral Treatments

Intensive behavioral treatments requires that children, parents, and teachers implement techniques that reward children for good behavior. The combination of methods aims to improve socialization, self-control, and academic abilities. Your child will attend school and willingly perform better by the end of intensive behavioral treatment.

Several intensive behavioral treatment summer camps are available, each lasting about eight weeks and perfectly timed before the school year. The typical mix of behavioral treatment and recreational activities at these camps ensures that the therapy is beneficial and enjoyable for the children.

## Combination of Pharmacological and Behavioral Interventions

Many ADHD children have benefited from a combination of medication and behavioral treatment in the past as it outperforms either behavioral or drug treatment alone. When both medication and behavioral therapy are used, therapists will usually reduce the times, doses, and medicines used during behavioral sessions. However, keep in mind that the individual patient will always determine the best use and combination of treatments.

## Effects of Medication on Children with ADHD

The impact of ADHD medication on motor activity and coordination is a significant side effect to consider. You may notice that your child's activity level in school has decreased due to medication treatment. It means he isn't running around as much as he used to. Additionally, you will notice an improvement in the neatness of your child's handwriting. We will see similar enhancements in other arts and crafts activities. Your children will be able to play with clay, building blocks, and other constructive toys more effectively.

In terms of cognitive effects, you will notice that your child has a longer attention span. He won't be as easily distracted in the future. He will be able to concentrate better on instructions. He will also experience a decrease in impulsivity and an increase in productivity. When he is asked to do something, he is likely to do it carefully and thoroughly. You will notice a significant improvement in accuracy and speed of work. When you consider the extent to which medication allows new information to enter your child's brain, you can see how beneficial meditation can be.

The most significant effect of any medication is its influence on social behavior. Being able to interact more effectively with others is critical in dealing with ADHD. Children on ADHD medication no longer gain attention in the classroom from other children or educators because their inattentive, off-task behaviors are reduced. When they interact with other people, they show less anger and are more self-control. Their social skills improve so dramatically that you can safely include your child in organized sports like basketball or soccer. Aggression and oppositional behavior are reduced, bossiness is eliminated, and such children begin to consider other people's perspectives.

Interpersonal therapies help people in regards to their relationships with others and their social abilities, i.e., how they usually relate to and interact with others. Many people seek therapy to address relationship issues, such as dealing with a separation or resolving a conflict with a loved one. Others seek treatment because they have become isolated or detached.

Another modality is comprised of medications, health and wellness, and biology. This method includes a variety of aspects, such as physical health and wellness (e.g., illness, health and wellness conditions, physical limitations, age-related health and wellness issues, chronic discomfort), organic factors (e.g., mind chemistry or genetics), and the requirement for drug or other types of clinical or organic therapy. This modality also includes a way-of-life routines that influence one's health, such as exercise (or lack thereof), diet regimen and nourishment, rest habits, alcohol, overindulging, and medication use, cigarette smoking routines, and so on.

The specialist in multi-modal therapy analyzes these modalities in two ways: by speaking with the client and having him or her fill out a questionnaire known as the multimodal life history inventory.

# Chapter 23:
# Techniques for Maintain Spiritual and Mental Well-Being

## How Spirituality Aids ADHD Symptoms

It Benefits Your Organization

Spirituality allows a person to connect to a higher and more profound sense of purpose and state. Spirituality enables you to maintain order amid chaos. Individuals diagnosed with ADHD frequently exhibit a lack of proper organization as a problem and symptom.

Another issue that people with ADHD frequently face is a lack of or insufficient system. When faced with life's day-to-day confusion, spirituality and spiritual exercises provide you with a framework and guideline to manage life's chaos. An individual's spiritual life gives him or her a mission—something to anticipate. As a result, he or she would strive to complete this mission and, in so doing, bring order to an otherwise chaotic and disordered life.

For example, belonging to a specific religious organization, such as a church, helps you work toward fitting into that organization's structure by doing activities like attending services, praying daily, reading the Bible, and singing hymns. The practice of daily rituals provided by your religion in collaboration with the group provides a structure that helps individuals with ADHD see life in a more organized and focused design.

Spiritual exercises such as prayer, thoughtful meditation, Bible reading, and songs of praise and worship to God may provide the soul with a deep sense of relief and calmness that allows him or her to set aside the world's cares and become much more focused.

Verses from the Bible can help a family cope with the symptoms of ADHD. Stories about Biblical characters such as David, Ruth, and Esther, for example, can serve as a source of inspiration and provide you with the audacity and bravery required to face tricky situations, particularly when you suffer from people misinterpreting you, as is often the case in the lives of people with ADHD.

Faith in God elevates your soul to a state or position that your mind and body cannot reach. When you are overwhelmed with feelings of confusion and are downcast in spirit, trusting that God loves you even when you are suffering and that He has a specific purpose for you will provide you with a lot of comforts.

Faith in God encourages you to work from the perspective that you are specially made and unique in the eyes of God and man. It teaches you that everything works together for good in the lives of those who love God, including people with ADHD. It would assist you in viewing your ADHD issue to an end. Rather than seeing your symptoms as an impediment, you see them as tools to help you get to where you need to go. This thought will assist you in learning how to manage it better and more appropriately.

Faith in God and prayer provide a child with ADHD with the inner grace and patience required to cope and deal with ADHD symptoms.

## Evidence of a Relationship Between Spirituality and ADHD

Some believe that spirituality and faith in God play an essential role in the healing and treating many common diseases. Studies have indicated that there may be a connection between spirituality and an individual's improved health and quality of life, and the quality of life of those closest to them. An enthralling study that looked at Americans' religious experiences showed that 100 participants discovered their involvement in religion significantly improved their physical health. The advantages of their faith in God extend beyond simply attending religious services.

Religious practices and faith transcend age and racial boundaries, in addition to improving people's well-being. Another study of African Americans discovered that people who participated in organized religious activities had better lives and were more satisfied. Those who engaged in religious practices outside of a collective structure also reported an increase in their sense of well-being and happiness.

A significant finding across many different racial groups revealed that practicing spirituality has a considerable impact on one's quality of life. Spirituality spreads like wildfire. It benefits not only the individual in question but also the rest of the community, including non-believers. It seems that communities are healthier when more people in that community live a life based on trust in God, and that emphasizes implicit obedience to God and his standards of behavior, the Ten Commandments. Non-believers benefit from their neighbors' spirituality because social norms favor traditional values and the healthier lifestyle pursued by their spiritually active neighbors.

After a thorough examination with appropriate lab or other essential medical tests, a doctor can provide a clear picture of the patient's health status based on the results obtained. The individual's health status, in general, determines what he or she frequently feels and experiences as the quality of life in day-to-day living. This health status is only a tiny part of the totality of the person's being. Other factors are far more critical to the issue at hand.

Furthermore, an individual's health is related to their habits. Consider a person who has developed the habit of eating red meat. The more red meat he consumes, the more cholesterol he accumulates in his system, increasing his risk of developing high blood pressure, heart disease, cancer, digestive problems, concentration problems, renal health problems, and renal failure.

Although this is true, there are a few exceptions where a person is raised in an environment that encourages them to eat a lot of red meat. An individual's habits as an adult are heavily influenced by the culture in which he grew up. However, there are cases where a person grew up eating red meat and whose parents are smokers and drinkers. Still, the person does not smoke, does not drink, and is a vegetarian. Such a person chose to work against the existing culture and practice different habits, allowing his personal choices and values to take precedence over the culture.

Finally, every individual's personal choices are influenced by much more than just the dominant culture. As a result, an individual's preferences and personal values are inextricably linked and dependent on his overall sense of the meaning and purpose in life.

There is a sense of being and purpose in life related to the individual's spirituality and faith in God. As a result, this illustration demonstrates that belief in God has a positive impact on health. That same trust directly impacts an individual's overall meaning and purpose, which influences his or her values and choices. Thus, personal values and preferences influence the culture they adopt, which directly affects the specific set of healthy habits that directly impacts their health and overall well-being. Trust in God, on the other hand, ultimately builds and strengthens health.

As a result, incorporating the spiritual element into the diagnoses and treatment procedure is critical for a holistic cure to be accurate. Trust in God is an effective treatment for ADHD symptoms. When children are raised with Godly values and a keen sense of well-being from an early age, it reduces their penchant for these abnormal behaviors and symptoms.

Some children are predisposed to ADHD, but with proper attention paid to their biological, psychological, social, and spiritual lives, it can be significantly helped if not cured.

## Chapter 24:
# Empowering Your Child: Tools for Dealing with Uncontrollable Stressors

From an adult's perspective, childhood might seem like a carefree time–full of playing, imagination, the ability to go throughout your day without worrying about a job, bills, and the constant demands of "adulting." However, children still experience stress in all areas of their lives. Things such as school and academic demands, social dynamics and peer pressure, and the lack of control over their daily lives can take quite a toll on a small human's developing mind, heart, and emotions—especially if there are not enough adults in their lives who are willing to listen and help them process through these challenging situations.

Parents and caregivers cannot protect children from stress, disappointment, or failure. However, they can help them develop healthy ways of coping and solving everyday problems. In fact, it can be freeing to look at things from this perspective even from infancy: it doesn't have to be our job to stop our babies from crying. Babies cry. Children struggle. Life is hard. It is our job, however, to hold our children through it—sometimes physically, sometimes mentally, sometimes emotionally, and sometimes in all ways.

There are plenty of types of stress in this world, and many of these can be positive stressors as they relate to the way they work with our brain and hormones. Positive stress can be the anticipation of a sports game, the unknown of learning a new skill, or the newness of changing schools and making new friends. When these types of events are talked about, prepared for, and processed (usually with positive outcomes), our brains and bodies see them as challenges that we have overcome and learn to anticipate that stress with an "I did it before, I can do it again," type of attitude.

However, oftentimes children are subject to more adult types of stressors that they not only don't have control over, but that they can't understand on their own. Stressful events can have effects on a child's well-being, especially when they are not processed or handled in a beneficial way. When children face uncontrollable stressors such as their parents' divorce, excessive pressure in school, moving, or feeling as if they don't have friends, their emotional and behavioral actions might be affected. Since major stressors in children are often chronic, some children might experience high distress levels for prolonged periods.

Adverse childhood experiences (ACEs) are a particular type of traumatic stress that can influence a child's development. Basically, the more ACEs a child encounters in their developmental years, the greater the likelihood that they will develop emotional and physical disorders and struggles. ACEs can include things such as abuse, neglect, or violence, witnessing abuse or violence against a loved one, or losing a family member to a negative or unexpected death. They could also include situations such as growing up in a home where the adults abuse substances, struggle with mental health problems, or where parental care is unstable due to prison, jail, or custody disputes. The more ACEs a child experiences, the more likely they are to have chronic physical, mental health, and substance abuse disorders. High levels of ACEs are also linked to lowered academic performance, fewer or less profitable job opportunities, and decreased earning potential.

Society itself, in addition to parents and caregivers, can strengthen their own families or those with whom they work in many ways. To strengthen economic support, it's important to have a household with financial security and to have a job with family-friendly policies. Parents should take part in public education campaigns against violence and adversity and teach men and boys to be allies against violence. Children who are given the benefits of high-quality childcare and enriching education often get off to a better start and are more likely to succeed if they are taught skills in social-emotional learning, safe dating and relationship practices, and if the parents approach family life with positive skills. Children and youth can be connected to mentoring and/or after-school programs when parents are not available. It's also important to normalize ACEs as something we all experience, and to be able to reach out to our communities to receive the services of individualized primary medical care, victim-centered services, treatments, and family therapy.

While exploring this area of childhood stress, adverse childhood experiences, and community resources to strengthen families, you can empower your children at home or in the caregiving situation by teaching them these three strategies: positive imagery and distraction, developing reasonable proximal goals, and reconstruing situations.

Reconstruing Situations

The way children interpret situations in their lives can play a vital role in their emotional reactions to those events. Parents can help children overcome feelings of distress and failure by helping them face the future with a positive attitude. Reconstruing a situation can be a positive way of coping with uncontrollable stress because it shifts a child's perspective from a pessimistic, self-defeating attitude to a more optimistic perspective. Reconstruing involves taking a situation that many would categorize as negative, and "flipping the script" so that it is empowering to that person's growth and development. It doesn't mean brushing things under the rug or ignoring struggles, but rather, processing them in a way to take charge of the situation and use uncontrollable circumstances to one's benefit.

When anyone, children especially, construe events or qualities about themselves in a pessimistic or derogatory way, they are more prone to passive behavior, withdrawal, and depression compared to those who choose to look at things from an optimistic and efficacious perspective. Children who tend to blame others and look for the negative in a situation, for example, thinking that others are always bullying or out to get them, are more likely to engage in aggressive behavior, as well.

Cognitive therapy has been shown to be beneficial for children struggling to interpret situations in a positive light. During these sessions, children are encouraged to identify negative thoughts and to challenge them with an opposing, positive viewpoint. The older a child is, the more help they seem to get from cognitive therapy focused on reconstruction, probably because they have greater metacognitive skills. Metacognition means "thinking about thinking"—the greater one's metacognitive skills, the more they can process situations in depth and see many sides of a situation.

One should be careful not to use reconstruction in a way that is maladaptive or taken to an extreme. For instance, a child who fights with others regularly and blames the conflict on everyone else would not be beneficial. Some others who are experiencing heightened forms of chronic trauma might create imaginary personas or misconstrue their lives into "other worlds." Although they might be self-preserving, it could be a dysfunctional coping mechanism.

## Skills That Might Be Lacking

Many of us have some skills that are weaker than others. They include:

- impulse control
- problem-solving
- delaying gratification
- negotiating
- communicating wishes and needs to adults or peers
- knowing what is appropriate or expected in a situation ("reading the room")
- self-soothing

Self-regulation is an important skill that should begin to be taught early in life. As humans, we cannot avoid difficult, negative, or unfortunate situations. Instead, the goal should be to learn how to navigate through them. For example, children can be taught to take an overwhelming task, such as cleaning a very messy room, into smaller, more manageable tasks. First, they could pick up the large things taking up a great deal of space, such as pillows, books, then dirty clothes. Then, they could put toys into piles: blocks, game pieces, and stuffed animals.

If a child is struggling with a physical task, instead of just expecting them to do the entire thing well on their own from the beginning, they could be taught and guided with the focus on one part first. Take brushing teeth: they could practice putting toothpaste on the brush and then the rest could be taken care of by the parent until the toothpaste skill is mastered. Then they could move on to brushing with their own hand.

When children act out when they are overwhelmed, frustrated, or in an unknown situation, the parent or caregiver can physically and emotionally get "down to their level" and encourage them to breathe, slow down, and reflect. The physical part is important: when we kneel, sit, or crouch down and look at a child in their eyes, we are less overwhelming to them and can be seen more as a partner as opposed to a towering authority figure. What is going wrong? What is hard? How can they be in charge of fixing the situation? Help them to name emotions and come up with a plan. Put some of the control back into their court and involve them in the process for growth.

Encourage mindful behavior. Mindfulness helps people to focus on the present, instead of brooding about the past or worrying about the future. Parents should practice this for themselves as well, so that they can be present in the situation with their child and see it as part of the journey, as well.

## Scenarios For Concrete Understanding

Here are some examples of children using these skills for beneficial emotional growth.

Positive Imagery and Distraction

Scenario 1: Shayne has not regularly seen a dentist over his eleven years of life, since as a young child he had a negative experience and has since expressed a phobia surrounding teeth and dental work. He has a cavity causing him extreme pain, however, and it needs to be filled. His parents involve him in the choice of a pediatric dentist, looking at pictures of the office and discussing what will be involved in the treatment. When they get to the office on the day of the filling, Shayne sits down in a chair that has a mural of outer space painted on the above ceiling. Shayne uses the distraction techniques he has practiced at home to "zone in" on the stars and planets and visualizes himself as the captain of a spaceship exploring new galaxies. Soon enough, the dentist is "bringing him back to Earth," and Shayne is pleasantly surprised at how painless the procedure was.

Scenario 2: Francis' family has recently moved into a new neighborhood in a less affluent part of town, and into a much smaller apartment than their old home. Her parents both lost their jobs during the recession and life is quite different now than it used to be. In the beginning, she was sullen and resentful, constantly "wishing she could just go home." Each night, when her mother or father was tucking her in to sleep, they would imagine beautiful, sprawling landscapes and visualize beautiful places in nature that they wished they could visit. At first, Francis did not participate on her own, but her parents kept modeling the practice for her and eventually she would jump in with her own ideas. Francis began drawing pictures of these places to hang on her walls, and would bring in flowers, nut and rock collections, and other pieces of nature to adorn their home. She learned to create a space in which she wanted to be.

Developing Reasonable Proximal Goals

Scenario 1: Chase's family is going through a divorce. Chase, a seven-year-old boy, is quite upset and often tells each parent that the other wants to get back together and "be a family again." Chase's mother acknowledges his feelings of upset and frustration but doesn't know what else to say. Finally, the parents sat him down together and explained, without vilifying each other, why it was healthier for the parents to live apart and that they both still loved Chase just the same. They suggested that Chase could come up with ideas to make his time with each parent as positive and enjoyable as possible. They made a list of the benefits to having parents that lived in two places, and although the negative emotions were allowed time in conversation and were continued to be addressed, the family tried not to make them the focus.

Scenario 2: Maddison was a teenager when she decided that she wanted to take up ballet. Although she had never danced before, seeing a community production of The Nutcracker inspired her to take up the hobby. At first, she was overwhelmed in watching the girls her age rise onto their pointe shoes and pirouette across the stage, and she also felt "babyish" taking the initial introductory ballet courses with the younger children. With the encouragement of her instructors and her parents, she decided to look up videos on strengthening the muscles needed for ballet, practiced on her own each day, and sought out classes for "older beginners." Maddison's instructor spoke frankly with her about the fact that her first few recitals would have "supporting roles," but they made a realistic timeline for dance goals and checked them off one by one.

Reconstrual

Scenario 1: Georgia has never been able to walk, due to a birth defect affecting her neurological and physical capabilities. In her early school years, she was angry about her situation and ashamed of the fact that she needed a wheelchair. She would often express that she wished she could "do what the other children did." However, in middle-elementary school Georgia had a teacher who saw an opportunity for empathy-building and reconstrual. Her teacher encouraged her speak to her classmates about the experience of being in a wheelchair.

Although she was initially nervous, Georgia began opening up when her peers expressed curiosity and interest in her "special chair." They began sharing ideas about how Georgia could participate in games and activities and wanted to help push her around the grounds. From then on, Georgia began to see her situation to gain individual attention in a positive way and as a conversation starter with new friends. She was more involved in peer activities and began to enjoy school much more.

Scenario 2: In an unfortunate riding accident, Jamel fell off his horse and broke his dominant arm in multiple places. He needed two surgeries and was going to be in a cast for months. Horseback riding had been his life, and he was devastated. Jamel seemed depressed after the accident, not wanting to participate in any other type of entertainment or activity. His occupational therapists began encouraging other types of ways to be involved with horses, such as going to the stables and feeding, grooming, and simply spending time with the animals, while strengthening his arms and fingers at the same time to prepare for the time when he could get back on a horse. His parents encouraged him to journal about his experiences and draw pictures about what he would do once he could get back to riding. Jamel had never been an avid reader or writer, or as interested in the other aspects of horsemanship, but after the accident he had many other ways to incorporate equine love into his life.

# Chapter 25:
# Calming an Explosive Child

We need abilities as parents, grandparents, and caregivers. We must keep trying something, anything, until we find something that will quiet an agitated child. Do not surrender. We'll look at some techniques you may use the next time your youngster loses control of their emotions. Both the caregiver and the child must learn to regulate their emotions. When a parent is in tune with their child and in control of their own body, they can use co-regulation to help their child cope with stress. Children learn to manage their strong emotions in tandem with a safe and supportive adult through co-regulation. If a child has been subjected to abuse and neglect, he or she may lack a mental model for self-soothing and emotional regulation. This is where you enter the picture.

It is your responsibility as an adult to offer a stable and loving environment for your child, tempered by tough and positive discipline. If you're also dealing with trauma, tiredness, or other mental health difficulties, this can be extremely tough to sustain. Therefore, it's so important for caregivers and instructors to look after their own emotional health. Nobody can pour from a cup that isn't full. Self-care has become a buzzword in this era, but what it truly means is that we must learn to control our own emotions to effectively parent or deal with children who have experienced trauma and loss.

When a child is enraged, remember that children never choose to have a meltdown, just as we wouldn't want to have a tantrum in front of our boss or parents. Explosive conduct in a child might activate the fear center in a parent's brain, causing us to react with annoyance rather than caring. When we are terrified, we frequently display rage. It is impossible to learn and connect when two individuals are in a condition of fear and wrath. The desire for connection and trust is ingrained in our DNA. Even though we are terrified, it is what we all require.

Fear or shame-inducing penalties and discipline should not be used to help a child with explosive behaviors because this will just lead to more outbursts. Explosive outbursts indicate that a child's brain has gone "offline." Children in this state are unable to hear you or comprehend the lesson you are attempting to impart about right and evil. This may appear ridiculous to you. You may assume that children must learn their lesson right now or they will grow up to be unruly and problematic adults. It's how many were raised—in a culture that employed rewards and consequences to coerce youngsters to comply in groups.

Many caregivers are trapped and unsure what to do because of new research on how to assist children recover after trauma. Most individuals before this age were raised with rewards and penalties, but for the many youngsters affected by trauma and terrible childhood experiences, this isn't working anymore. We need to try something new, and change is difficult. Our brain saves energy by making automated decisions based on previous experiences, especially when we are stressed. According to the findings, nearly half of today's children find sanctions and rewards ineffective.

But there is reason to be optimistic! Understanding the mechanics of anxiety and stress in the body necessitates a paradigm shift away from rewards and consequences. To assist children with extreme behavior in reclaiming their identities calm, I devised a step-by-step strategy!

## Go from Chaos to Calm

1. Keep track of when the behavior occurs most frequently and see if you can predict the trigger or cause.
2. Pay attention to a child's initial signs of tension or worry. Fast or repetitive speech, self-soothing behavior such as fidgeting, walking in circles, rocking, jumping, or any strong energy/movement are all early symptoms of distress. If you pay close attention, you will sense it in your own body.
3. Ground yourself once you've identified the source of your anxiety. Remind yourself that the youngster is in distress right now and that you must remain calm. Even though it feels like an eternity, staying calm is the fastest method to calm a child's worry.
4. Allow some time to pass between your realization and your response. Use affirmations or take a minute to imagine yourself successfully dealing with their anxiety. Consider how much better you'll feel if you can maintain your composure in the face of adversity. There is no remorse.
5. Determine whether they child requires assistance to settle down or securely expressing their biological need to move. Calm the body first, then the mind. Anxiety causes us to become more

active. Telling a child to sit or relax is ineffective. Time out isn't going to help. Find a safe way for them to move their bodies. Trampolines, pillow fights, and leaping on the bed are all possibilities. You are not rewarding poor behavior; rather you are assisting your child in regaining emotional control and returning their brain to a receptive learning state before attempting to connect on a logical level.

6. Check in with them after some energy has been expended and inquire whether their body feels finished with the exercise. If this is the case, provide calming play activities that engage the senses. They'll be drawn to arts and crafts they've never tried before. Taking a walk outside to play with chalk, swing, or gaze up at the skies. Before trying ideas, find out what their body requires to feel better. Allowing the youngster to select the relaxing activity will help them develop emotional intelligence.
7. Once their body has calmed down, connect with them, and try to communicate with them. This isn't about succumbing to unpleasant habits. When the child's body feels less worried and comforted, they will be more able to hear and learn from the lesson you wish to teach them.

You can retain your limits and say NO firmly without losing your cool if you follow these instructions.

We may never be able to handle every eruption correctly, but if we can improve the number of times we get it right, the emotional climate in your family or classroom can change dramatically.

# Chapter 26:
# Autism Spectrum Disorder - A Checklist of ASD Red Flags

## The Disorders within the Autism Spectrum (ASD)

The disorders included in ASD are as follows:

Autistic Disorder

Children affected by an autistic disorder face issues forming normal relationships and communicating with others. Their range of interests and activities is limited. Symptoms vary greatly between patients. Strangely, the numbers of boys affected by an autistic disorder are five times that of girls.

Asperger Disorder

Asperger syndrome affects more boys than girls. These patients have normal intelligence, and their language capabilities develop early. However, their social skills are impaired, and they cannot communicate effectively with others. Children with Asperger's are known to have poor coordination, repetitive speech, difficulties with reading comprehension, math, written skills, obsession with some specified topic, and lack of common sense.

PDD-NOS

Pervasive Developmental Disorder-Not Otherwise Specified (or also known as PDD-NOS) is called atypical autism. It is a neurological disorder that has some but not all attributes of Autistic Disorder. Children with PDD-NOS are known to have severe impairment in several spheres of development.

Childhood Disintegrative Disorder

Also called Heller's syndrome, this condition occurs in three- to four-year-olds. The child's intellectual, social, and language skills are met at in an age-appropriate timeframe, but and deteriorate over several months. Symptoms include loss of social skills, loss of bowel and bladder control, loss of motor skills, delay or lack of spoken language skills, inability to start and sustain oral communication, and so on.

Rett's Disorder

This is seen in girls (mostly) between the ages of 6 and 18 months. It is characterized by wringing of the hands, slow head and brain growth, seizure, walking abnormalities, and mental retardation.

Children diagnosed with ASD face difficulties in the following areas:

- Communication and language
- Socialization
- Restricted interests
- Impairment in social collaboration
- Lack of eye contact
- Lack of warm, cheerful expressions
- Lack of interest or happiness
- Lack of reaction to their name
- Impairment in communication
- Lack of indicating signals
- Lack of coordination of nonverbal correspondence
- Unusual prosody
- Limited inflection and pitch
- Unpredictable mood
- Surprising voice quality
- Repetitive behaviors and restricted interests
- Repetitive developments with items
- Repetitive movements or posing of the body

Within the above areas, ASD patients manifest many different symptoms. Therefore, two different ASD patients usually have a distinct set of behaviors and abilities.

The range of ASD symptoms is a broad one. Some speak in single words or short sentences, while some have great verbal skills. Some children are less sociable and like to be alone, while some like to socialize, but face challenges in socializing.

These children have a wide range of interests and repetitive behavior. Some children have an interest in unusual things like signboards, street signs, animals, plants, and gardens. Some have made a hobby of collecting unusual objects like pencil sharpeners and erasers.

In some cases, the interests of these children may not be appropriate for their age or in terms of the intensity. For instance, a child has a knack for detailed information on a particular topic, and sometimes, they are known to have an extreme interest in only one item, such as an unhealthy interest in one toy above all others.

Another common observation is that they have repetitive behaviors and/or mannerisms. They may be simple behaviors like the flapping of their hands or a more complex mannerism. The list is endless as each child diagnosed with ASD is unique, and no two behave in quite the same way. Therefore, there is the need for personalized care for each ASD patient.

Roughly 1 out of every 85 children is born with ASD and boys are 5 times more likely to be affected than girls, going by the numbers. If you think your child may have Autism Spectrum Disorder, please read the rundown of conceivable indications of ASD.

Your child does not have to exhibit the greater part of the shown practices to allude to for an appraisal. Kindly note that these qualities might likewise be markers of different conditions as well as conceivable early indications of ASD.

If your child demonstrates two or a greater number of these signs, please approach your pediatric doctor for a referral for an assessment. A screening apparatus called the M-CHAT (Modified Checklist for Autism in Toddlers) can help you determine whether you should seek an expert opinion.

There is a unique form of autism, Savant syndrome, in which individuals have outstanding aptitudes in particular areas. They include music, craftsmanship, and numbers. Individuals with this type of autism perform these abilities without practice or lessons.

Due to the nature of the symptoms, Autism Spectrum Disorder is sometimes challenging to diagnose at an early age. If the parents have no experience with autism, they may see other babies and toddlers develop differently and begin to worry. When expressing these concerns to relatives, friends, or neighbors, the parent will often hear things like, "The child will grow out of it." Parents will sometimes talk to their doctor about their concerns about their child's lack of verbal communication and eye contact, inability to respond to their name, and their obsessive attachment to specific objects.

In many cases, a baby will develop naturally and then begin to regress at around eighteen months. These children are generally easier to diagnose due to the apparent difference in past and present behaviors that parents and professionals can attest to by looking at photos, watching videos, and comparing observations. Some children have chronic ear infections; others may show allergic reactions. Many have intestinal problems: chronic diarrhea or chronic constipation. Or a child may have constant anger or sleepless nights.

Parents may be concerned because their child is a walking encyclopedia on a particular topic (such as trains), obsessively playing the same toy the same way, or only eating certain foods. Perhaps the kindergarten teacher notices a child who doesn't seem to engage in conversation with classmates and struggles with any changes in routine. Maybe a child is considered "bad" at school because of certain behaviors. The child might just be developing at a slower pace that others, but it's best to be safe and investigate your concerns.

The physician may hesitate to jump to any conclusions because not all reported observations are objective and may have alternate interpretations. Everyone knows someone who talked late. On the other hand, a parent may not listen to concerns expressed by a childcare worker, teacher, or neighbor. It is unfortunate because the earlier the diagnosis, the better the prognosis. Some people with Autism Spectrum Disorder can reach adulthood without ever being diagnosed. They may have always felt like they weren't in harmony as others from a social, emotional, or sensory standpoint.

## Behavioral Characteristics of the Autism Spectrum Disorder

- As a child, he or she does not reach out to be held by their mother or seek cuddles
- They do not imitate others

- Use the adult to obtain the desired object, without interacting with the adult as a person
- Does not develop age-appropriate peer relationships
- Lack of spontaneous sharing of interests with others
- Difficulty mixing with others
- Prefer to be alone
- Are detached from the feelings of others
- Little or no eye contact
- Does not develop speech or develop an alternative method of communication such as pointing and gesturing
- They have the word, and then lose it
- Uses repeated words or phrases instead of everyday language
- Speak on very narrow topics
- Difficulty speaking abstract concepts lack or impairment of conversation skills
- Inappropriate attachment to objects
- Strange obsessive play with toys or objects
- Dislikes change in routine or environment
- Will only eat certain foods
- Will only use the same item (same plate or cup, same clothes)
- Repetitive motor movements (rocking, hand flapping)
- Distinctive vocal characteristics (flat monotone or high pitch)
- Does not reach developmental milestones in a time frame or neurotypical sequence
- Low muscle tone
- Irregular fine and gross motor skills
- Cover their ears
- Does not respond to noise or name; they act deaf
- Does not react to pain
- Becomes stiff when held, dislikes being touched
- Becomes hyperactive or unresponsive in noisy or very bright environments
- Eat or chew unusual things
- Picks objects up to smell them
- Often removes clothes
- Hits or bites themselves (hitting the head or slapping the thighs or chest)
- Hits or bites others
- They have tantrums for no apparent reason, and are difficult to calm

- Lack common sense
- Doesn't seem to understand simple requests
- Frequent diarrhea, upset stomach, or constipation

Many of these behaviors are the children's responses to how they are processing their surroundings.

Different analysts are exploring the likelihood that under specific conditions, there may be a mental imbalance. Still, different analysts are researching issues during pregnancy in addition ecological elements, for example, viral contamination, metabolic lopsided characteristics, and exposure chemicals.

- **Genetic vulnerability:** A mental imbalance tends to happen more often than anticipated among children who have specific medical conditions, including delicate X disorder, tuberous sclerosis, innate rubella disorder, and untreated phenylketonuria (PKU). Some unsafe substances ingested amid pregnancy additionally have related to an expanded danger of Autism.
- **Ecological factors:** Examination shows different variables other than the hereditary segment are adding to the ascent in expanding event of autism—for instance, ecological poisons like exposure to metals such as mercury, which are more predominant than previously noted. Those with autism (or those in danger) may be vulnerable against such poisons, as their capacity to metabolize and detoxify these exposures may be compromised.

## Parent Involvement

A collaborative partnership between home and school can be a blessing. Frequent opportunities for discussions and feedback about the child's individual learning needs can indeed make a big positive difference to your child's life. Make sure you are in regular touch with the school.

Explosive students have trouble transferring or generalizing knowledge and skills from one situation to another. Of course, the child gains most because of collaboration between home and school. For the explosive child, it means that the same skills and concepts are reinforced at home and school, leaving little opportunity for confusion. A lack of this kind of coordination might bring a lot of confusion to the child's life, often having to learn a separate set of instructions at home and school.

These are the main types of valuable information that parents and teachers can share:

- The developmental history of the child.
- Any important health issues.
- Information about the range of professionals and caregivers that have been involved in caring for the child.
- Likes, dislikes, sensory sensitivities, and special interests of the child.
- Knowledge about effective positive reinforces and motivators that work with the child.
- How the child has learned a particular skill at home.
- Behaviors and strategies that have been successful at home or in other environments.
- Performances as students over brief and prolonged periods and different settings.
- Perspectives on the student's perspectives, and other useful information.

It is important to consider the format, information that needs to be shared, and other information that may be needed from parents on a day-to-day basis at the school. There should be strict guidelines for reporting any significant behavioral changes or events that need mention between home and school. Generally, the classroom teacher is responsible for the content of home-school communication. You may consider it a daily diary for the student. Things that should be included in the diary are like:

- Activities in which the student participated.
- Any new skill that was demonstrated to the child.
- The nature of play with classmates.
- Songs and stories of the day.
- New areas of learning.
- Upcoming events, trips, or any special interactions/participations.

A child diagnosed with Autism Spectrum Disorder is a major impact on the family. In addition to the stress associated with bringing up a child who needs more attention and care, children with autism are not as friendly as other children and do not approach their parents in the same way as other children. This lack of spontaneous signs of affection from one's child is difficult for a parent. Families often tend to isolate themselves due to concern about their child's socially inappropriate behavior or fear of being embarrassed by certain behaviors of the child or the extreme fatigue that most parents of children with Autism Spectrum Disorder suffer. Families stop doing what they did before. Single-parent families find themselves alone, with their hands full, with no free time to continue living any kind of social life, increasing their isolation. Being a single parent, adoptive parent, stepparent, custodial parent, or grandparent raising a child with Autism Spectrum Disorder adds even more difficulty to an already precarious situation.

A marriage or relationship may deteriorate in response to additional stress, fatigue, and differences of opinion about how to handle certain situations. Often one or both parents have a tough time coming to terms with having this child and are in different parts of the pain cycle. Add to that, seeking support and trying to get proper education for the child and it's easy to see how many couples end up divorcing as a result.

Siblings may suffer from being raised in a family with a child who has Autism Spectrum Disorder. Not only do they have a sibling who is difficult to understand, with limited interests, and is not social; they also must put up with some pretty wild behavior. They feel the stress their parents are under and the fact that inevitably more of the parents' attention is occupied by the sibling with Autism Spectrum Disorder. However, research indicates that there are also positive aspects of having a sibling on the spectrum.

Extended family members, such as grandparents, also have difficulty dealing with Autism Spectrum Disorder. Some refuse to face the facts; others don't know what to say or what to do. Again, as a parent, it is up to you to decide when and what information to share.

# Guideline for Parents: Things You Have to Do to Support Your Child

Learn More about Autism Disorder

The more you think about a mental imbalance range issue, the better prepared you'll be to settle on educated choices for your child. Teach yourself about the treatment choices, make inquiries, and take part in all treatment choices.

Accept Your Child

As opposed to concentrating on how your mentally unbalanced child is unique and what he or she is "missing," practice acknowledgment. Appreciate your child's exceptional idiosyncrasies, praise little triumphs, and quit comparing your child to others. Feeling unequivocally cherished and acknowledged will help your child more than anything else.

Try Not to Give Up

It is difficult to foresee the course of a mental imbalance range issue. Try not to make a hasty judgment about what life will be for your child. Like others, individuals with a mental imbalance have a whole lifetime to develop and build up their capacities.

# Chapter 27: ADHD Symptoms and the Nature of the Disorder

## What Is ADHD?

Attention-Deficit Hyperactivity Disorder (ADHD) is one of the most common mental disorders affecting children. ADHD additionally impacts lots of adults. Signs of ADHD consist of inattentiveness, hyperactivity, and impulsivity.

An approximated 8.4% of children and 2.5% of adults have ADHD. ADHD is usually diagnosed in school-aged children when it brings about disruption in the class or troubles with schoolwork; it is more common among boys than girls, and it can, likewise, impact adults.

Living with ADHD can be tough both for the parents and for the children. The good news is that it's possible to live very happily even with ADHD. As you are learning in this book, there are plenty of things you can do as a parent to help your child grow healthier, stay more focused, and, generally, be better, both during childhood and as future adults.

Let's tackle what it doesn't mean. ADHD is not just a medical name for a child with a bit more energy than usual. All children have plenty of energy and that's a sign they are healthy, both mentally and physically.

However, when the energy is misplaced, too much, and prevents the child from learning, growing up, and living a life similar to that of other children their age, it can become a problem. Children and even teens with ADHD often have problems controlling their impulses, and paying attention are being one of the most obvious signs.

Such habits influence their schooling and life at home and their interaction with siblings and others. When this problem persists into adulthood, the adult with ADHD will display other signs such as having trouble managing time, establishing priorities, and holding down a job. Problems with relationships, possibilities of addiction, and having low self-esteem may also plague adults with ADHD.

## Causes

Overall, it is unclear what truly causes ADHD. Each case is unique and can differ from the next. What your child is experiencing might be completely different than what another child is going through. According to research, genetics plays the biggest role in the cause of ADHD. It is much more common for a child to develop the disorder when it runs in the family. Since it is hereditary, this is not something that should be considered contagious or transmissible. For example, if your child is playing with other children in school, there is no risk of them passing ADHD on to those children.

Scientists are still investigating how ADHD develops and what causes the disorder. There is plenty more research to be done. To date, they conclude that the genes present that typically lead to the development of ADHD include ones that are linked to the neurotransmitter dopamine—this is known as the neurotransmitter responsible for your memory, attention, and regulating body movements. Other research suggests exposure to certain chemicals as a child can contribute to the risk factor of developing ADHD. This theory is not definitive but is thought to be a possible link to the disorder.

Those who do not monitor their children's sugar intake or technology time still need to be much more cautious. Above all, ADHD is a brain-based biological disorder. There is nothing that you can do to fully prevent this from happening to any child, even your own. The good thing is that many children who develop ADHD can still be very high-functioning individuals.

## Symptoms of ADHD

The symptoms of ADHD vary from child to child but usually include a mix of hyperactivity, inattention, and impulsivity.

Inattention

It is not that children with ADHD cannot pay attention; they have no problem concentrating and staying on task while they are doing things they like or listening about topics they are interested in. They rapidly tune out when the job is monotonous or uninteresting.

Another typical issue is staying on track. Children with ADHD frequently jump from task to task without finishing any of them, or they skip stages in required processes. They have difficulty organizing their homework and time than other children their age. When there are multiple distractions around them, children with ADHD have difficulty concentrating; they typically require a calm, quiet atmosphere to stay focused.

The following are the most common indicators of inattention:

- Easily distracted and having a limited attention span
- Making thoughtless errors—such as in homework
- Unable to concentrate on arduous or time-consuming activities
- Displaying an inability to listen to or follow directions
- Unable to follow an activity or endeavor that is continuously changing
- Struggle managing daily chores
- Frequently avoids, resists, or is hesitant to undertake things that demand sustained mental effort
- Frequently misplaces items required for jobs and activities (e.g., school materials, books, pencils, eyeglasses, tools).
- Prone to becoming distracted

Hyperactive

Hyperactivity is the most evident symptom of ADHD. While many children are naturally energetic, others who suffer from (ADHD) hyperactive attention deficit disorder are constantly going. They may attempt to accomplish many tasks at once, jumping from one activity to the next. Even when made to sit motionless, which might be difficult for them, they tap their foot, shake their leg, or drum their fingers.

Hyperactive children appear to be constantly moving. They cannot sit still and will often run about or chat nonstop. Children with ADHD find it difficult to concentrate in class. They are likely to move about the room, wriggle in their chairs, twitch their toes, touch anything, or tap a pencil loudly. Children with ADHD may experience extreme restlessness.

The following are the most common indicators of hyperactive:

- Frequently fidgets or taps their feet and hands or squirms in their seat. In circumstances where being seated is anticipated, the child often departs the seat.
- Children find it difficult to sit still, play quietly, or relax. Move about a lot, probably running or climbing improperly.
- Excessive talking have a short fuse or a quick temper
- Frequently unable to play or participate in leisure activities in silence
- Frequently answers before the question have been fully answered

## Diagnosis of the Symptoms

Tests administered to diagnose ADHD looks for conditions within three unique sub-types, signs that arrive along a spectrum of intensity, and overlapping comorbid conditions that often complicate analysis and treatment. It takes intense evaluation to diagnose someone with ADHD. While an assessment for ADHD typically begins with a visit to the doctor, they rarely end there. Generally, most doctors are not trained to diagnose ADHD and its symptoms, and your pediatrician will refer you to a specialist.

Worthwhile ADHD diagnosis would depend on the criteria described in the Diagnostic and Statistical Manual of Mental Disorders, fifth edition (DSM-5). The specialist will delve deep into the patient's medical record and the results of a neuropsychological screening. These resources give insight into the patient's strengths and weaknesses and helps identify other conditions, if any.

Many doctors explain that some patients' ADHD symptoms aren't noticed until later in life—this is true for people who have the inattentive type of ADHD. Diagnosing a grown-up is trickier than diagnosing a youngster. The DSM-5 sign guide is not useful in adults; almost all its steps are meant for diagnosing children. An ADHD medical diagnosis in adults takes place in a careful and scientific observation conducted by an ADHD specialist who takes his/her time during the evaluation.

Recent research implies that in some people, symptoms are not obvious until adolescence when self-management problems surface in. Doctors may also diagnose adults who have just 4 or 5 symptoms if the symptoms are critical.

## Associated Conditions of ADHD

As if a diagnosis of ADHD is not enough for a parent to worry about, there are often other conditions that develop in conjunction with ADHD or only as a reaction to ADHD. Children with ADHD and an associated disorder require much more time, attention, and medical care. It is believed that about half of all people with ADHD also have another need. The Centers for Disease Control and Prevention estimates that about 2/3 of ADHD children have another disorder in children. Associated conditions can be mild or severe. They might be linked to ADHD, or they might be in a condition that has simply taken its time to show up and announce its presence. These additional conditions fall within two categories: secondary conditions and comorbid conditions.

Secondary conditions are those that are a direct result of ADHD. When a child is dealing with ADHD, it is quite frustrating and stressful. In many cases, other conditions develop because they are triggered by frustration and stress. As treatment of ADHD progresses, these secondary conditions often become more manageable or fade away entirely.

Comorbid conditions are conditions that exist concurrently with ADHD. They do not fade with ADHD treatment. Instead, comorbid conditions usually need a specific treatment program. You and your child's doctor must determine which additional conditions are secondary or comorbid.

The number of associated conditions a child or adult can have along with ADHD is endless. However, it is essential to know some common disorders and their possible symptoms because knowledge is power for ADHD. While not an all-inclusive list of probably related conditions, the following list describes many more prevalent associated conditions:

Anxiety

We have all felt a little anxious at some point in our lives. Anxiety manifests itself as feelings of stress, worry, tension, tiredness, and several other symptoms. However, the fleeting pressure the average person feels is not considered a disorder. Chronic anxiety affects about

30% of ADHD children and approximately 50% of ADHD adults. These feelings of worry and stress can have a detrimental effect on the nature of life. Whether or not the anxiety begins to diminish with ADHD treatment determines if it is a secondary or comorbid condition.

Depression

Everyone feels sad from time to time. Depression, however, is a severe disorder that involves handling unhappiness, moodiness, irritability, and even worthlessness. These feelings do not go away. Depression affects more than just your mood—it reduces your interest in life. It requires treatment, often including therapy. Depression may occur because of ADHD or because of environmental factors and genetic predisposition. In most cases, it is considered a comorbid condition.

When children have difficulty functioning, particularly when they have challenges at school due to ADHD, they may feel depressed and hopeless. As a result, people with ADHD have trouble paying attention and organizing them, exacerbated when sadness is present.

Comorbid depression affects around ten- to fifteen percent of children with ADHD. Due to a loss of self-worth, these patients frequently develop suicidal thoughts.

Learning and Language Disabilities

Many children with ADHD have a type of learning disorder. Dyslexia and dyscalculia are two of the most common learning syndromes that may affect an ADHD child. Dyslexia has an impact on the child's ability to read and write. Dyscalculia impacts the child's ability to understand and perform math skills. Language disorders affect ADHD children four times as often as non-ADHD children. Both learning and language disabilities fall into the category of comorbid conditions. They each require their treatment plan.

Gross and Fine Motor Skill Difficulties

Fine motor skills include tasks like grasping a pencil with your fingers and writing. Gross motor skills include physical activities, such as jumping and running. Both types of motor skills require the use of certain sets of muscles, which ADHD can affect. For example, you may notice that your child struggles to write neatly because his/her hand

and fingers jerk around. Your child may seem awkward and overly clumsy, such as falling frequently or struggling to do a jumping jack. These disorders are comorbid conditions and require their treatment plan.

Obsessive-Compulsive Disorder

The obsessive-compulsive disorder, also known as OCD, may have you thinking of the hoarding shows on television. While hoarding may be a symptom of OCD, it is not the only symptom. This disorder can be mild or extreme. It can manifest itself in repetitive behavior, like counting to a certain number while performing a task or even pulling out hair. OCD can also involve the extreme need to be clean, such as washing hands repeatedly, even until the skin is raw. OCD may manifest as hoarding, the overwhelming desire to collect certain items, or as an extreme anxiety to the point of being overly cautious. OCD is also a comorbid condition. Treatment can be helpful, along with possible medications.

Oppositional Defiant Disorder

The oppositional defiant disorder (ODD) is a common condition associated with ADHD. This disorder results in extreme bouts of anger and rage that is not a typical temper tantrum. Rather, it is an uncontrollable anger/outrage that occurs during a meltdown that results from even the smallest trigger. These meltdowns may last a few minutes or as long as half an hour. When an ODD child has a breakdown, he or she is usually quite remorseful about what happened once calm again. This disorder can be secondary or comorbid, and there are diverse types of treatment available.

Bipolar Disorder

Bipolar disorder is another mood disorder that has various symptoms. It is a comorbid disorder, so you cannot expect ADHD treatment to fix the bipolar problem. Bipolar disorder often includes severe and unexplainable mood swings. For example, your child may be ecstatic and extremely happy for several days, only to suddenly switch gears to anger and rage that also lasts for several days. People with bipolar disorder have a tough time relaxing and calming down, especially when they are in a manic state of mind. There are numerous medical treatments to help control bipolar disorder because even though the highs a patient feels is significant, the lows may feel worse than anything they have ever felt—possibly driving them to the point of suicide.

Tic Disorder

A tic disorder involves the physical twitching of certain groups of muscles. These muscles are often found in the face, neck, and shoulder areas of the body. You may notice short, jerking movements of your child's head, or rapid and uncontrolled eye blinking or a chronic twitch at the corner of the mouth. Tics are most often noticed in children, and many outgrow the disorder by adulthood. It was once believed that certain stimulant ADHD medications caused tic disorders. However, more has been learned about these types of conditions, including the fact that there is a genetic factor to consider. It is now believed that the stimulant medications did not cause the tic disorder. The drug flipped on the internal, genetic predisposition switch residing within the child. Tic disorders are comorbid disorders and can be managed with appropriate treatment.

Tourette Syndrome

Tourette Syndrome is one that most people misunderstand. A person hears the word Tourette, and they automatically assume that the afflicted will randomly yell out swear words. That is not a movie—this is real life. It is interesting that many who suffer from Tourette Syndrome also have ADHD. Tourette syndrome does vocally manifest itself. Think of it like tics, and only it is tics of the vocal cords. People with this disorder may make odd noises randomly or repeat phrases indiscriminately, including the occasional swear word. However, uncontrolled swearing is not a realistic description of Tourette syndrome. That is a comorbid condition that requires a different treatment plan than ADHD.

Substance Abuse

Often, children with ADHD have a higher risk of cigarette smoking at an early age, and as much as twice the likelihood to develop and addiction. They also have an added chance of following nicotine dependence with alcohol abuse and, in severe cases, drug abuse. Interestingly, children with ADHD who are treated with stimulant medications are less likely than their non-ADHD peers to abuse illegal stimulants, such as cocaine and methamphetamine. That may be a result of the opposite effect that stimulants have on ADHD children. These substance abuse problems are a secondary result of ADHD. In many cases, with the appropriate treatment, parents can be proactive and prevent substance abuse from ever becoming a problem by actively treating ADHD.

Conduct Disorder

Conduct disorder (CD) is a pattern of conduct in children who repeatedly violate others' rights or basic social standards. The child often displays these behavior patterns in several contexts, including at home, school, and in social interactions, and they cause considerable impairment in social, academic, and familial functioning. An elevated level of uncontrollable aggressiveness characterizes this condition. Children with CD are more prone to injure themselves and others severely. They have a propensity for breaking regulations and causing intentional harm to others' belongings.

It's thought that approximately a fourth of children with ADHD have been identified with at least one behavioral or conduct disorder. Early treatment, as usual, may make a dramatic difference.

Mood Disorders

ADHD individuals have a co-occurring mood disorder in about a third of all cases. Extreme mood swings are a symptom of mood disorders. Children who suffer from mood disorders may appear to be in a poor mood all the time. For no apparent reason, they may weep every day or be angry with others regularly. Depression, bipolar illness, and seasonal allergies have been more frequent in persons with ADHD of all ages. It is critical to keep an eye out for indications of these diseases and get treatment if necessary.

Autism Spectrum Disorders

Autism Spectrum Disorders encompass a wide spectrum of conditions marked by difficulty with communication, social skills, routine changes, repetitive behaviors, and how children perceive different senses. Many of the symptoms that are found in ADHD are also observed in ASD. It is believed that around a third of children diagnosed with ADHD also fulfill ASD criteria. Furthermore, having an

ADHD diagnosis has been proven to postpone the diagnosis of Autism by up to three years.

## Treatment of Conditions Linked with ADHD

When a child has both ADHD and a co-occurring disorder, a health care provider may choose to treat the ADHD first since primary treatment of ADHD can reduce stress, increase attentional resources, and improve the child's capacity to manage the signs of the other condition. Medication, behavior therapy, skill training, counseling, and educational supports and adjustments are all possibilities for ADHD treatment. These treatments can be customized to the children and family-specific requirements. They can assist the patient in controlling symptoms, coping with the condition, improving general psychological well-being, and managing social interactions.

# Chapter 28:
# What is the Distinctive Between ADD, ODD, and ADHD?

## The Difference Between ODD and ADHD

People with ODD (oppositional defiant disorder) exhibit persistently negative, hostile, defiant, disobedient, and destructive behavior. They frequently react negatively to authority figures who try to direct, question, or correct them; defiance of authority figures is a distinguishing feature of ODD. People with ADHD may also be defiant and argumentative to gain attention. They rarely see the connection between their behavior and its consequences for others. They rarely recognize the emotions or thoughts of others. People who suffer from ODD set a poor example by being manipulative, taking advantage of others, and showing little or no concern for how their actions affect others. People who have ADHD perform worse in school, are less successful at work, and can be destructive or aggressive as children and later in life.

When either ADHD or ODD symptoms affect different settings, there is a significant difference in hyperactivity. ADHD typically manifests in all environments (school, home, etc.), whereas ODD manifests primarily in negative social behaviors with others. ADHD affects more people and is more prevalent. Anger in people with ODD may be associated with negativity. Individuals suffering from ODD must be hostile to notice their insecurities and genuine feelings of inferiority. They often feel that it is necessary to prove their worth to others, frequently in negative terms. People with ADHD may also be attention seekers, but their anger affects them more than their family or others.

## Problems Commonly Associated With ADD

Children with attention deficit disorder (ADD) may have learning disabilities and experience distress due to repeated disciplinary issues, even in college. Adults and peers may conclude that such students are sluggish due to their inattention to jobs and failure to complete tasks thoroughly. Many parents and teachers fail to recognize ADD as a possible cause of their children's academic and social difficulties.

Instead, they are likely to see the student as a naughty child. Potential employers may interpret the child's inattention and lack of focus as shyness or a lack of commitment to tasks. He or she may also show signs of a short attention span, a lack of listening, a long attention span, forgetfulness, difficulty planning, and a lack of motivation and perseverance. In general, people with ADD are accused of having poor grades or having difficulty at work because of these characteristics.

## Basic Characteristics of ADHD

As stated in the Diagnostic and Statistical of Mental Disorders, attention deficit hyperactivity disorder (ADHD) is classified as an "attention-deficit disorder, primarily inattentive demonstration."

ADD will not manifest itself in the same way as a hyperactive-impulsive type of ADHD. Students in this situation exhibit a variety of symptoms. Children who have the additional two signs of ADHD, for example, tend to have behavioral issues as a result. Children who have attention deficit hyperactivity disorder (ADHD) are not disruptive in college. They could even sit quietly, of course.

Nonetheless, this does not mean that their disorder isn't a problem or that they aren't struggling to focus. Furthermore, not all children with ADD keep their desks, locker spaces, and their assignments disorganized. They may drop materials at college, misplace schoolwork, or fail to submit projects. It may irritate educators and parents, resulting in the child receiving low grades in the course. Behavior therapy can be used to combat the child's forgetfulness.

Why Does ADHD Occur?

Though the exact causes of ADHD are unknown, certain factors play a role in developing this disorder. Let's explore some of them.

- **Inherited:** ADHD can be inherited. If either parent has this disorder, their children are at risk of inheriting it. Certain genetic traits are passed down through generations. A child who has one parent with ADHD has a greater than 50% chance of developing it, and a greater than 40% chance of developing it if an older sibling has it. However, the inheritance of ADHD is far more complicated, and it is not due to a single genetic flaw.

- **Pregnancy Issues:** ADHD can develop because of specific pregnancy-related issues. A child who is born prematurely or slightly underweight is more likely to develop this disorder. A child whose mother has experienced complicated pregnancies is also at risk of developing this disorder. Your brain's frontal lobe oversees the control of emotions and impulses. As a result, children who sustain head injuries in this region are more likely to develop this disorder. Pregnant women who consume alcohol or smoke are more likely to have a child with ADHD. Exposure to pesticides, PCBs, or lead during pregnancy may also increase the likelihood of the baby developing ADHD.
- **Brain Functions:** If a child develops an infectious disorder that affects the brain tissues, such as encephalitis or meningitis, it may affect the child's ability to send signals after birth. It may also cause ADHD symptoms.

The neurotransmitters, chemicals found in the brain, function differently in adults and children with ADHD, even how the nerve pathway's role varies. Specific brain areas in ADHD children are smaller or less active than those who do not have this disorder. Dopamine, a neurotransmitter, also plays a vital role. It's associated with learning, attention, mood, sleep, and movement.

Brain activity differences have been found in people with and without ADHD, according to studies. The precise significance is still unknown.

- **Other Considerations:** Few groups of people were thought to be at a higher risk of developing ADHD than those born prematurely, that is, before the 37th week of pregnancy. People who have epilepsy are more likely to develop ADHD as are those with brain damage. This damage can occur in the mother's womb or from a severe head injury later in life.

Types of ADHD

Hyperactivity, impulsivity, and inattention are hallmarks of ADHD. Most people who do not have ADHD have some degree of impulsive or inattentive behavior. But people with ADHD have severe hyperactivity-impulsiveness and inattentiveness. There are three types of ADHD, and each is associated with one or more characteristics.

- **Predominantly Inattentive ADHD:** People with this type of ADHD primarily exhibit symptoms of inattention, and their impulsiveness or hyperactivity is not as significant. Although they may struggle with impulse control, these are not the primary characteristics of predominantly inattentive ADHD. Girls are more likely than boys to suffer from this type of ADHD.
- **Predominantly Hyperactive-Impulsive ADHD:** People with predominantly hyperactive-impulsive ADHD suffer from other symptoms in addition to inattention. Patients with this pattern may be inattentive at times, but this is not the primary feature of this disorder. Children with this disorder can cause a lot of disruption in their classroom. They make learning much more difficult for both themselves and other students.
- **Combination ADHD:** When a person has combination ADHD, their symptoms do not fall neatly into hyperactive-impulsive behavior or inattention. Instead, they have a mix of symptoms from both categories.

## Detecting ADHD Symptoms at Every Age

Symptoms are not enough to diagnose ADHD, but they are vital warning signs that can help you identify the problem and treat your child. In general, childhood ADHD symptoms include a combination of hyperactive, reckless, and impulsive behavior. If the symptoms appear in at least two different settings over six months, a diagnosis was made. But did you know that the symptoms of ADHD change with age? Here are some general guidelines for determining whether your child requires medical attention and an ADHD evaluation.

This disorder can be detected in the pre-school years, although a diagnosis will be more difficult because children in this age group are typically excited and inattentive. ADHD symptoms become more noticeable when children begin school and must be present in a structured environment. They might be unable to follow simple instructions, sit down, or wait their turn. They may talk constantly, move, and switch from one activity to another. Please keep in mind that several developmental disabilities share these symptoms, so make sure your child's doctor performs a thorough evaluation rather than simply reviewing the list of symptoms.

ADHD symptoms in the school environment become more noticeable during the primary school years. Children with combined type ADHD and hyperactive ADHD tend to get up from their seats, talk over, or blurt out answers during discussions. Those with inattentive ADHD are much more difficult to detect. They are typically well-liked children with mediocre grades, a result of difficulty completing homework or following instructions. They spend more time dreaming in class than paying attention, and they avoid tasks that require sustained concentration. They may also be the most disorganized students in the class.

ADHD can remain undetected through the high school years; if the child is clever enough, they can compensate for their symptoms. Nonetheless, secondary education presents a significant challenge to children with ADHD due to increased workload and responsibilities. Schoolwork is not the only issue; ADHD was frequently associated with other problems such as low self-esteem, eating disorders, and risky behaviors such as drug experimentation and casual sex. Because distinguishing between typical adolescent mood swings and ADHD symptoms can be difficult for parents, seek professional help if you notice significant changes in mood, socialization, or school performance.

Attention Deficit Disorder Hyperactivity Symptoms in Children

According to some studies, the top ten factors of ADHD sleep disorders are why some people can't sleep at night. Many people with ADHD sleep problems stay awake in bed for two to three hours before falling asleep. Stress causes difficulty sleeping and can result in other forms of psychological and physiological imbalance, leading to depression and other conditions of mental problems in the patient.

The bad news is that many parents are hesitant to seek ADHD treatment for their children because they may blame themselves for their child's behavior. You must understand that it is not anyone's fault because the problem is inside the brain. If you suspect your child has it, please seek treatment as soon as possible.

Few children with ADHD symptoms are treated. If left untreated, it can harm your child's future. He or she is likely to drop out of school, struggle to make friends, and struggle to keep a job. Don't let your child become a victim. ADHD children are easily distinguished from normal healthy children. Children with ADHD have symptoms such as being unable to focus, being unable to remain calm, being unable to stay in a seat, and frequently having behavioral issues that cause problems at school and home.

Stimulants are commonly used to treat this disorder. When children with ADHD are given motivations, they can make better choices, are not repulsive, and do not engage in risky behaviors. They are less likely to be rough than neglected or abused children.

Interventions such as short-term goals, reinforcement, and consistent boundaries and consequences, in addition to treatment, will help the child learn how to control their behavior.

# Chapter 29:
# Prioritizing a Healthy Diet: What to Eat and What to Avoid

Your daily diet encompasses all the foods and supplements you take and should help your brain function well and reduce symptoms, such as restlessness or inability to sustain concentration.

Focus on making good choices:

- Overall nutrition. The assumption is that the foods you eat will make your symptoms better or worse. You might not be eating some foods that might help you get better.
- Supplements. With this, you add nutritional supplements, nutrients, and vitamins to your diet. The theory is that it could help you make up for the inadequate nutrient. It is believed that if you don't get enough nourishment, it could worsen your symptoms
- Remove certain foods. This involves not eating foods or things that trigger your symptoms or worsen them.

**Top Foods for the Explosive Disorder**

- Additive-free and unprocessed foods. Due to the harmful nature of additives, you should eat fresh and unprocessed foods. Additives include artificial sweeteners, preservatives, and colorings which can be found in processed foods, they are detrimental to explosive children.
- Chicken. Tryptophan is an important amino acid that aids in the body's protein synthesis and serotonin production. Serotonin induces sleep, happy emotions, and helps with impulse control and hostility.
- Eat breakfast. For most children with explosive disorders, breakfast helps the body regulate bloodstream sugars and stabilize hormonal fluctuations. Eat breakfast that has at least 20 grams of proteins. Try smoothies with 20 grams of proteins; they are a delicious and filling way to "break the fast."
- Wild-caught salmon. It is not only rich in vitamin B-6 but is also filled with omega 3. It is thought that omega-3 solved learning

and behavioral problems (like those related to explosive disorders). Individuals, including children, should eat healthy salmon at least twice a week.

## Foods to Avoid

- **Sugar.** This is the main trigger for children. Avoid any type of refined sugar including chocolate, desserts, soda, or fruit drinks.
- **Gluten.** Some researchers and parents observe worsening behavior when a child eats gluten, which can indicate sensitivity to the protein in wheat. Avoid all foods made with whole wheat grains such as bread, pasta, and whole wheat grain cereal. Seek out gluten-free and even grain-free alternatives.
- **Milk products.** Most cow milk contains A1 which may trigger the same reaction as gluten and should be avoided. If severe symptoms occur after consuming milk products, discontinue use. Goat's milk doesn't include proteins and it is a better option for explosive children.
- **Food color and dyes.** Children may be allergic to food dyes and colorings; therefore, all processed foods should be avoided. Colorings and dyes can be found in nearly every commercially prepared food. Food dyes can be found in energy drinks, chocolates, wedding cakes mix, chewable nutritional supplements, and even toothpaste!
- **Caffeine.** Although some believe that caffeine might help with some behavioral disorder symptoms, it pays to lessen or avoid caffeine. The side-effect of caffeine, include anxiousness, and nervousness. All these can further worsen the explosive symptoms.
- **MSG and HVP.** These additives are believed to lessen dopamine amounts in children and adults. Dopamine is from the brain's pleasure and prize systems. For children battling with behavioral explosive disorders, well-balanced dopamine is essential.
- **Nitrites.** Commonly found in lunch meat, canned foods, and some processed foods, nitrites are connected with a child's growth, type one diabetes, certain types of malignancy, and IBS. It could result in an increased heartbeat, difficulty breathing, and restlessness that aggravate explosive disorders symptoms.

- **Artificial sweeteners.** Artificial sweeteners are harmful to your health, and for dealing with the behavioral disorder; the unwanted effects could be damaging. Artificial sweeteners create biochemical adjustments in the body, which can affect cognitive function and psychological balance.
- **Allergens/things that trigger allergies.** Eliminate the top seven allergens, including soy, wheat, milk, peanuts, tree nuts, eggs, and shellfish. Furthermore, eliminate any foods or drinks that are personal contaminants in the air. This may include papaya, avocados, bananas, kiwis (for people with latex allergies), coriander, caraway or fennel (all the same family), and chocolates.

## Supplements for the Explosive Disorder

Some experts advise that explosive children need 100% vitamin and nutrient supplements each day. Other diet experts believe that individuals who take balanced meals don't need a supplement or micronutrient supplements. They claim there is no scientific evidence that vitamin or mineral supplements help all those with the disorder. While multivitamins would help for children, teens, and adults who don't balance their meals, consuming more than the daily dose of vitamins could be toxic, and should be avoided.

Symptoms of explosive disorder differ from person to person. Work closely with a medical doctor if you're taking supplements. To help yourself, identify the food that is making your symptoms worse and endeavor to eliminate it from your diet. If the symptoms disappear, ensure you avoid the food and avoid it entirely.

If you cut out your favorite food from your daily diet, does your symptom worsen? Research is ongoing in this area, and the details aren't clear.

Iron Supplements

More studies are being conducted that show the effects low iron can have on children. When we think of a lack of iron, we think of those that are suffering from blood loss. When our bodies are lacking this basic mineral, much can happen, including an increase in our explosive disorder symptoms. An iron deficiency affects more than you might expect.

Iron is important to our bodies because it is what is responsible for making sure that oxygen makes its way to our vital organs and all our muscles. We also need it for proper brain function. When we lack iron, it can also slow the production of dopamine, which is essential for those that want to live a happy, healthy life. If our explosive symptoms are out of control, then it might be a sign that we need more iron in our lives and diets.

Omega 3/6

Recent research has found that increasing our intake of healthy fat, such as that found in omega-rich meals, can aid in the normal generation of dopamine in our brains.

These fatty acids will improve brain function. While doing this, they will also increase attention. When brain function and attention increase, explosive disorders symptoms dramatically decrease. Along with more attention, these supplements can also help lessen restlessness, impulsivity, hyperactivity, and overall aggression in children. Some scientists even believe this is the best treatment for those that don't want to use any other medications.

Most researchers don't recommend this technique for controlling explosive disorder; however, here are some common concerns and what professionals suggest: Food additives: In 1975, an allergist initially proposed that artificial colors, flavors, and preservatives might trigger hyperactivity in a few children. Child behavior experts have extensively argued this matter. However, one research demonstrates that food color and preservatives do increase hyperactivity in some children. However, the effects vary with age and type of additive.

Sugars: Some children become hyperactive after eating chocolate or other sugary foods. No study has proven that this triggers explosive disorders; however, sugary foods are best avoided.

Children that were given fish oil supplements were found to be better at reading and spelling, with overall improvements in their behavior as well. This means that children can benefit greatly from including this supplement in their diet. In addition, it is one of the top natural depression fighters out there. As adults, we get even more health benefits from improving our omega-3 and -6 fatty acid consumption beyond just the reduction of our explosive disorder symptoms. These include an increase in eye health and a lower risk of heart disease developing.

# Chapter 30:
# Options for Handling Problems: Three Plans

Before continuing, it's a good idea review what's already been discussed. A lack of flexibility/adaptability, frustration tolerance, and problem-solving abilities are all symptoms of learning impairment. This emphasis also allows us to pinpoint the exact cognitive abilities that need improvement and personalize therapy to the individual requirements of each child and their caregivers.

For this reason, we suggest that a child's lack of cognitive abilities is just a partial explanation for their issues and that they are more likely to explode when they interact with others who have different temperaments. Finally, by emphasizing situational specificity, we can show that the factors that lead to explosive episodes are extremely foreseeable and may therefore be addressed well in advance.

These factors have been included in a framework known as the *three baskets* earlier (this term came from the initial days of the CPS model). The *plans framework* has many uses, but we'll start with the most basic: assisting parents in recognizing their choices for dealing with difficulties or unfulfilled expectations in their children, as well as how these options influence their connection with the child and the child's behavior.

## Three Cards

While adults may react to challenges or disappointed expectations with children in a variety of ways, the plan model divides them into three groups. The first approach, dubbed *plan A*, is forcing an adult's will. In other words, grownups are adamant about having their expectations satisfied. Of course, this is an exceedingly popular choice. The second alternative, dubbed *plan B*, is including the youngster in a collaborative effort to address whatever problems or obstacles are preventing expectations from being reached (this option is not very popular but happens to be one of the main focuses of this book). *Plan C*, the third alternative, is lowering or eliminating expectations.

Depending on the child's needs and skills, as well as the adult's objectives, all three may be successful answers. As we work toward the objectives of minimizing explosive episodes, enhancing adult-child relationships, and teaching deficient cognitive abilities, we use this basic framework to assist adults to begin to classify and reflect on their own conduct, as well as reassess and prioritize expectations. By the way, the most popular misconception about the CPS model is that it forces adults to put all their hopes on hold. Since the CPS model holds that people who have high expectations for children are beneficial, this must be established early on. A crucial therapeutic consideration involves the realistic nature of the child's goals and expectations. Each plan shows diverse choices for reacting when reasonable expectations are not reached. Let's take a closer look at plans A and C.

When a youngster fails to fulfill expectations, it's normal for adults to become more adamant that the child conforms. For example, if a child was not cleaning his or her teeth at night as per the parental expectation, plan A would include a more extensive request that the child brush his or her teeth. This persistence is often based on the notion that the youngster did not understand the significance or need of the expectation, or that the child needed a little prodding. The child does not have a severe response to the intense persistence, and the child fulfills the expectation (having understood its value or recognized the meaning of the little additional push).

However, imposing an adult's will (plan A) on a youngster with explosive tendencies increases the likelihood of an explosive episode and, as a result, has serious negative consequences. The issue with plan A isn't that people are pursuing their goals, particularly if the goals are realistic (meaning the child can reach the goal continuously). Using plan A puts children at greater risk of having explosive outbursts since it is based on adult expectations rather than child needs. In other words, the traits of a particular child and the method in which adults pursue their expectations are incompatible from a transactional standpoint.

Many adults react to this mismatch by escalating plan A's application, frequently by offering rewards or proposing punishment, intending to provide children with a greater desire to respond to plan A adaptively. The child's bad reaction to plan A is just a trained method of compelling adults to surrender or succumb.

The notion of "giving in" to the youngster is naturally unappealing to the adults. The fact that such a mindset is so deeply established in American society (but not in other cultures) means that adults who adhere to it have never given the topic any consideration or been introduced to a cognitive viewpoint on children's conduct, and thus they lack any other tools in their discipline repertoires. Adults may use the CPS model to think about the issue more deeply and challenge commonly held beliefs, as well as to be exposed to a cognitive viewpoint and to get assistance.

1) Recognize that there are three approaches to dealing with difficulties or disappointed expectations in children.
2) Acknowledge it.
3) Acknowledge that, given their child's cognitive qualities, one of the other two response alternatives may elicit it better outcome.

## Options for Handling Problems

Parents have generally handled such challenges and unfulfilled expectations using plan A, and Plan A is such an established and cherished part of our society for many individuals (including many professionals), that many folks are not aware of when they're employing it. As a result, we often find ourselves having to assist children identify while they are expressing their will or adopting an intrinsically rigid posture.

"No," "You must," "You can't," and "1... 2.... 3...." are some popular plan A entrance phrases. Unlike some other therapy modalities, the CPS method does not put a premium on educating adults on how to implement plan A effectively. Indeed, the CPS approach actively seeks to assist people in resolving difficulties and achieving their goals by using plan B instead of plan A. Plan C is the last option.

Plan C entails lowering or eliminating a certain expectation. Plan C is quite helpful in lowering a child's overall frustration level. When adults say nothing or just indicate that they don't object to a child's request or conduct (e.g., "OK"), they are indicating that they are implementing plan C. Plan C, for instance, in the situation of a youngster who refuses to clean their teeth, would normally include removing the demand entirely. It's worth noting that when adults use plan C, they accomplish their aim of minimizing the chance of an explosive episode. However, keep in mind that the aim of following what one considers to be an essential adult requirement (toothbrushing) is not met. We never know how adults would react when we recommend that certain expectations be managed using plan C. Some people are pleased that someone in authority is allowing them to lower or remove assumptions about which they may have had doubts. Others are concerned that employing plan C would result in the expectation not being realized.

Adults typically require reassurance that most of the reasonable expectations that were temporarily put on the "back burner" early in therapy will make their way back into our talks after the child's issues are thoroughly understood, and the stability of the family has improved. Let it be noted that, in most cases, cleaning one's teeth is a reasonable expectation. Without first determining if (1) there are legitimate (possibly motoric, sensory, or emotional) challenges interfering with the child brushing his teeth, or (2) the child is so, one would not begin to consider the value of this expectation, and how it can be addressed if it is not fulfilled.

## Explosive Child Care

Impaired in the realms of frustration tolerance and flexibility, adding one more demand or annoyance to the mix breaks the proverbial camel's back at the end of a long day. Plan C is quickly defined by many adults who are unaware of the CPS paradigm as "giving in," defined as when an adult starts managing an expectation with plan A and subsequently switches to plan C due to the child's negative reaction. When an adult starts with plan C, the adult is simply emphasizing that an expectation is not currently being pursued, maybe because the other expectations are stronger in the hierarchy or because the expectation has become unrealistic because of a better knowledge of a child's issues. Plan C is sometimes confused with ignorance by other, uninformed adults. The two words are not interchangeable. Ignoring, when used as a behavior control tactic, is an attempt to divert adult attention away from or encourage certain behavior. Plan C simply signifies that an adult has decided not to continue a certain expectation.

## Intervention Goals

Adults are striving to involve the child in a working process toward a mutually satisfying resolution of adult and child issues with plan B. However, we're going to skip over this choice for now to focus on a few key issues. The CPS model delineates three key intervention aims since it was initially intended for the treatment of particularly challenging children and adolescents. One objective is to cut the number, severity, and length of explosive episodes in half. With plan C, you may reach this aim by dealing with a lot of adult demands. Psychotropic drugs may be beneficial for accomplishing this objective when certain pathways (mainly emotion control and executive abilities) are implicated. Plan B is also exceptionally good at preventing explosive outbursts. Plan A, on the other hand, tends to trigger violent outbursts.

A second purpose of the intervention is to assist individuals in achieving their goals. This aim may be achieved using two plans concurrently, most often plan A and B. Adults use plan A to achieve their goals by expressing their will, typically at the expense of causing an explosive outburst. Adults are likewise following their expectations with plan B, rather than forcing their will to complete the mission, they are collaborating with the child to find a mutually acceptable solution to the obstacles conflicting with expectations being fulfilled. The same expectations that may be continued with plan A can be continued with plan B as well.

The third purpose of counseling is to educate missing cognitive abilities. Both plan A and plan C will help you achieve your objective. In other words, neither the imposing of adult will, nor the deletion of adult expectations successfully train the cognitive impairments covered by the routes. Plan B is a successful method of teaching such abilities. Indeed, only plan B can help us accomplish all three intervention objectives at the same time: fewer explosive episodes, mature expectations, and the training of missing cognitive abilities. As a result, the success of plan B—that is, assisting adults and children in working collaboratively is critical.

Because they have yet to identify the limits placed on their child by the pathways, many adults overemphasize plan A (imposing of will) before and early in therapy. These people are often preoccupied with the validity of the expectations and the potential negative consequences for the child's growth and long-term result if they are not met. Typically, such people are both the cause and the victim of explosive outbursts. These adults can be reassured that their concerns are valid ("Yes, Juan must brush his teeth"), but they should also consider whether (1) the expectation is realistic at this stage in the child's development, or (2) whether there are ways to pursue the expectation without causing explosive outbursts. High dependency on plan A might also originate from the frequent misconception that pursuing expectations in this manner is more efficient or quicker. What's the use of talking to a child when you can simply tell them what to do?

Plan A is faster on the front end. Plan B, on the other hand, is more efficient overall and the hours spent problem-solving together is often far less than the time spent dealing with a child who has gotten out of hand and becomes aggressive or destructive. In other terms, explosive incidents (caused by plan A) usually take longer to resolve than long-term difficulties. Adult expectations are unreasonable in certain circumstances, and they must be examined. These discussions center on whether a child's ability to satisfy certain expectations is hampered by cognitive skill deficiencies.

For example, imagine we've determined that a child's fluctuating cognitive set is a source of vulnerability. We discovered (via our situational analysis) that a youngster had frequent explosive outbursts on weekends. After more investigation, we discovered that the child's weekend itinerary is set up in such a manner that frequent switching from one activity to another is required. Adult persistence (plan A) is not strengthening the child's ability for shifting but is producing numerous explosive episodes. This will require that parents shift their mindset about how the weekends are planned (plan A) and will also need to work with their child to help them learn how to make shifts without becoming upset (plan B).

If a youngster brushes his teeth as frequently and thoroughly as his parents want, the expectation has been satisfied, and the plans are no longer necessary. If a youngster is completing his homework as well and as consistently as his instructors would want, the expectation has been reached, and the plans are no longer required. But if a child isn't brushing his teeth, doing homework, doing chores, or getting along with his classmates or siblings, those are unmet expectations, and you now have three options: impose your will, drop the expectation, or collaboratively solve the problems and teach the lacking skills that are interfering with the expectation being met.

Of course, how one informs (or reminds) a child of an expectation can result in an explosive outburst before any plan can be implemented. "Get your butt in that kitchen and do the dishes," for example, would be a fairly inflammatory way to express an expectation, whereas "Don't forget about the dishes" would be closer to the mark.

Plan C, on the other hand, isn't something you use all the time; it's something you use exclusively for certain difficulties or triggers, right? Right. Plan C will be used on certain triggers, while plan B will be used on others. So, without adopting plan A, is it feasible to address disappointed expectations and solve problems? It's not just conceivable—it's likely. But there's a lot more to see to it than what you've read so far.

# Chapter 31: Other Practical Recommendations for Assisting Your Child in Coping with the Demands of Daily Life

A child with ADHD has difficulty with day-to-day tasks that other children appear to breeze through. These practical tips can help your child cope better:

## Make a Structure

When your child performs tasks in expected places and at scheduled times, they will find it easier to focus, concentrate, and complete them. They require predictability, comfort, and structure.

Create and maintain this structure at home. When your child is familiar with the situation and understands what is expected of him, he is more likely to perform well.

## Create a Routine

Make routines for play, homework, meals, and bedtime. Make them straightforward and predictable.

Teach your child, for example, to prepare their school supplies before going to bed and have the child put them in a certain location. He is less likely to be anxious when he wakes up in the morning. He is aware that his belongings are prepared. He is mindful of their location.

## Assist Him Keep a Time Record

Make use of clocks. They serve to remind of the things that need to do at specific times.

Reduce complexity.

Consider his abilities concerning the specific demands of the activities in which you want him to participate.

Suppose you force him to commit to more than he can handle. In that case, he may become distracted, nervous, and "wound up," rendering him ineffective.

Allow him sufficient time to complete assigned tasks so that he does not panic or give up.

Make use of charts.

Charts can serve as visual reminders for tasks that your child is expected to complete, such as daily chores, homework, special assignments, and so on. If the task is enormous, divide it into smaller chunks so your child does not become overwhelmed.

Make the chart exciting and appealing. Make use of color-coding. Make it a point to decorate it with stars or points for good behavior.

## Create Checklists

Suppose your child finds any task (usually one with multiple steps) stressful or complicated. In that case, a checklist will serve as a memory aid, allowing him to feel in control and organized.

For example, make a list of everything he needs for any given school day and tape it to his door.

Children should use a timer.

A child who has ADHD has a short attention span. They become agitated when they must concentrate for what appears to be an extended period.

To address this issue, set a timer for 15 or 20 minutes each time there is homework. When the timer goes off, your child should take a brief break before setting the timer for another 15 minutes.

When your child knows there is a quarter-hour break, they will not become bored or give up. Homework will appear to be more tolerable.

Make a quiet and private space in which he feels at ease.

If your child is in a relaxed, comfortable, and quiet environment, they will focus better on his homework.

## Maintain a Clean and Organized Home

A child with ADHD has difficulty staying organized. Keep your home neat and managed to set a good example. Your child will feel more at ease if things are easily found when they are needed.

## Make Rules for Your Home

Direct your child that you expect them to adhere to specific rules and expectations. Make the rules clear, simple, and understandable.

Write down these rules on a large sheet of paper and hang it on the wall so your child can easily refer to it whenever he needs to.

Create a straightforward system of rewards and consequences. Sit down with your child and go over the effects of obeying or disobeying the rules.

Maintain consistency. Follow through on what you've said. Carry out the agreed-upon reward or consequence.

Keep your child away from situations that are too challenging for him to handle.

When you put your child in a situation for which he is not emotionally prepared, he may react violently.

If you know he gets easily agitated and impatient, don't make him wait for prolonged periods. If he has a temper tantrum when he doesn't get what he wants, don't take him to a store where the variety of toys is likely to overwhelm him.

Encourage him to express his feelings when he is upset.

Finding the right words to express his emotions will deter him. It will reduce the desire to act out. It also makes him realize that he can better control his impulsive behavior by taking the time to reflect on and express his feelings aloud.

## Use Timeouts

A timeout can be used as an appropriate punishment for inappropriate behavior. It is a firm, brief, and acceptable method of instilling discipline.

A timeout can stop your child's out-of-control behavior. It neutralizes it, allowing your child to regain control. It is the proper method of teaching your child to accept the consequences of his actions.

## Assist Him in Making Friends

Children with ADHD are frequently easy prey for teasing. They talk too much, say inappropriate things, interrupt frequently, are unable to read social cues, and often appear indifferent or overly intense or aggressive.

Many ADHD children, on the other hand, are brilliant and wise. When left to their own devices, most children can figure out how to make friends with the right children. Furthermore, some children are likely to find their quaint ways endearing and amusing.

It is always a good idea to assist your child in learning social rules and skills.

Sit down with your child and explain their unique challenges to them in a gentle but direct manner. Make suggestions for how they can make changes.

Show them how to be a better listener. Teach them how to read body language and facial expressions by teaching them cues. Educate them on how to interact with peers more easily.

Role play. Consider a variety of social situations that they are likely to encounter. Change roles. Make exercise enjoyable.

Assist them in making friends with children who have similar physical abilities and languages so they feel at ease with these children. Begin by inviting only one or two friends at a time. When they play, keep a close eye on them. Bullying, yelling, pushing, or hitting will not be tolerated.

Allow them space and time to enjoy the game. With a smile or praise, reinforce good play behavior.

## Demonstrate Your Love for Them

Your child must understand how much you value and love them. You may end up hurting your relationship if you only focus on correcting inappropriate behavior. The child may come to believe they are unloved, undeserving, and underappreciated, and their self-esteem may suffer even more as a result.

Seek ways to boost his self-esteem.

Each child has unique talents and interests which parents should promote.

Every small success contributes to a child's self-esteem. Martial arts classes, music lessons, or art projects are often beneficial to a child with ADHD. Learn about your child's interests. Find out where they excel. Then look for an activity in which he is likely to excel.

## Be Generous in Your Praise

Children with ADHD are frequently chastised for their behavior. They are commonly subjected to complaints, corrections, and criticism for nearly everything they do or do not do.

Make a different choice. Think positive and be generous with your compliments.

Concentrate on your child's appropriate behavior rather than his or her inappropriate behavior. Every time they complete a task, no matter how minor, give a smile or share a positive comment. Keep in mind that what comes naturally to another child may be difficult for a child with ADHD. Thank them for his efforts.

Encourage them to think aloud while also encouraging people to wait their turn.

You may be wondering why on earth anyone would recommend encouraging a child with ADHD to think aloud. Isn't that one of the most severe issues? Indeed, children with ADHD frequently speak out of turn or act without permission, causing schisms in their environments and settings such as school or public spaces. When your child is in one of these settings or even at home, they are expected to follow a specific set of instructions. When they speak or act out of turn, they usually do not follow the instruction and end up in trouble. So far, we seem to be on the same page.

Thinking aloud, however, is a little different. You've probably seen your child get into trouble because they act or speak rashly. However, by encouraging your child to think aloud, you can better understand their thought process and, as a result, help them control their impulsivity. Waiting for their turn before speaking is an essential skill that can be taught alongside thinking aloud.

Once you and your child have worked on moderating their impulsivity, you can begin to teach the skill of learning to wait their turn, which is essential for the rest of their life. As you are likely aware, children with ADHD lack self-control. As a result, often, they are acting, speaking, jumping, dancing, throwing things, and everything else under the sun before thinking through their possible consequences.

Children with ADHD rarely can process their thoughts or actions before speaking or acting on them. It is these actions of interrupting or knocking over supplies that most likely earn results in numerous behavioral write-ups in your child's take-home folder and a rapidly declining behavior grade. Learning to think through consequences is an essential skill that your child will need to adapt to be successful students and eventually competent adults. To further understand this skill, one technique is to encourage thinking out loud.

When your child is encouraged to think out loud, you stop them before they interrupt or misbehave. You ask them to walk you through their thought process to tell you why they would do what they were about to do. For instance, if they are about to throw a toy at their sibling, you will stop them before this happens and ask them why they thought throwing a toy was an appropriate response to the frustration that they were feeling. You might ask, "What did your sibling do to make you angry?" Your child may not be able to answer this right away, which is where your help comes in. Try to help them find the words to communicate the emotion that they're feeling. A particular feeling prompts the action of throwing. Perhaps that emotion is anger, frustration, sadness, melancholy, or even embarrassment. Your child is probably already aware of some of these emotions. Still, it's your job to connect the action they were going to take with the feeling they felt to analyze what they were feeling and learn how to address that emotion better.

# Chapter 32:
# Physical Health Maintenance Techniques

Exercise and movement will provide you and your child with a wide range of options. It will also allow you to choose activities that will help you improve specific ADHD symptoms.

## Recreational Activities in the Outdoors

Sports for Individuals

Because your child may find team sports difficult due to his ADHS symptoms, you may want to consider individual sports instead of assisting your child in succeeding more.

If your child enjoys sports, he can participate in a variety of exciting and enjoyable individual sports, such as:

- Self-defense techniques
- Tennis
- Wrestling
- Swimming
- A game of bowling
- Playing table tennis
- Skateboarding
- Roller skating
- Ice skating
- Track and field events

Your child's natural high energy and enthusiasm will help them succeed and become a champion in these types of sports!

Suppose your child expresses an interest in an individual sport and wishes to enroll in classes. In that case, it is a good idea to take him to observe a class before enrolling.

Don't push it! If your child realizes they aren't enjoying the chosen sport, don't pressure them to continue. Instead, tell them that they "will learn to enjoy it when he gets better." You may be correct but putting pressure on your child will most likely make him dislike it even more. Children with ADHD are more likely to be passionate about something for a brief time before losing interest.

Similarly, if you believe that your child's abilities are ideal for a particular sport, don't pressure him if the sport isn't appealing. Allow your child to make suggestions and make the final decision.

Whatever individual sport your child chooses to participate in will be an excellent way to channel his energy. It will help them control their ADHD symptoms, focus better, develop social skills, and sleep better.

## Indoor Recreational Activities

Once the weather does not allow outdoor activities, you must provide a variety of indoor activities to keep your child busy and give him an outlet for his energy. Indoor activities should ideally adhere to the following basic guidelines:

- Indoor activities for children with ADHD should be structured.

The structure is essential to children with ADHD. They need to know what will happen next, what to expect, and how to act in each situation.

What am I going to do?

The structure must be laid out for them in the form of planned activities. It includes telling your child what needs to be done, providing the necessary materials, and clearly stating the solution to winning or succeeding. For example, tell the child to color an entire coloring book page in three different colors.

- Indoor activities should stimulate as many senses as possible. You have used the child's feelings of touch and sight in the preceding example.

Multisensory activities aid in the child's concentration. Among the multisensory activities are:

- Food preparation
- Tabletop games
- Playing cards

- Construction with Legos
- Hula hooping
- Coloring and painting
- Play-Doh
- The Twister
- Jumping rope
- Volleyball with balloons
• Indoor activities should include movements. Naturally, this is not always possible with all games. Determine whether you need to structure-activity with more (or less) action based on your child's energy and mood. Alternatively, combine activities such as dancing with quieter activities such as board games or video games. Keep in mind to schedule time for these activities as well.

Indoor activities can include both group and individual activities and activities with more movement and quieter ones. Here are some more ideas:

- Hide and seek
- Singing and dancing
- Playing charades
- Creating cookies
- Construction
- Using an acoustic device to listen to audiobooks
- Arts and crafts
- Scavenger hunts
- Singing
- Obstacle courses

Now that you've gotten the idea come up with some activities of your own to keep your child active and engaged on rainy days!

## Therapy Through Play

Play therapy is an excellent tool. It is used in many psychotherapy and child psychology areas to assist children with disabilities in developing skills while having fun.

You can have your child participate in play therapy with a specialized child psychologist. Still, you can also use this method with your child at home.

Therapeutic Art

This type of therapy assists children in developing their creative abilities and expressing themselves through the medium of art. The child is asked to paint or draw something, describe their day at school or an enjoyable event, or even draw themselves as they feel.

The child's artwork may reveal specific issues that he is experiencing, allowing parents or the therapist to discuss them further. Furthermore, it is a fantastic way to keep the child-focused while exploring and developing his creativity and uniqueness. Here are a few ideas:

- Making a collage out of old photos or magazine images
- Creating a postcard with a short message to send to someone the child is angry with or wants to thank
- Creating a digital slide show with photos of the child that make him or her happy (or sad)
- Responding to music; listening to a short piece of music, and drawing on how the child is affected
- Use window markers to decorate a window
- Finger painting
- Creating a self-portrait
- Creating a drawing for a special someone
- Drawing with your eyes closed

## Play Therapy Activities and Games

Experts believe that inexpensive and straightforward play therapy techniques can help parents help their children with ADHD make significant gains. Traditional games such as Clue and Let's Go Fish are also beneficial.

Depending on your child's age and the specific area you wish to assist him in, you may want to consider the following options.

Games of Imagination (Ages 4-6)

Children with ADHD frequently struggle with expressing and channeling their emotions. Fantasy play is critical for teaching children with ADHD how to express themselves more effectively when they are angry or frustrated.

How Should Play Therapy Be Structured?

Set specific times. Play sessions should last 10 to 15 minutes to avoid boredom; however, if the child remains interested in the game for longer than that, continue!

While the child is playing, prompt them. For example, if you're playing with a puppet named Fred, begin the game by saying, "One day as Fred was walking to school..." or "Once upon a time, there was..." You can also prompt your child during the game by acting out a role in the game.

During the game, encourage good social behavior. "What will happen if the doctor yells at the sick person?" or "How will the little girl feel if her friend refuses to share?"

Here are some ideas for fantasy play:

- Dolls are fun to play
- First-aid kits
- Han and his finger puppets
- Animal stuffed toys
- Action figures as well as monster figures

Developing Life Skills (6-10)

These skills are critical to developing at this age because they will stay with your child for the rest of their life. They include learning to deal with frustration and anger, wait their turn, and complete assigned tasks. Games that help build social skills include:

- Let's Go Fishing
- The Memory Exercise
- Ladders and Chutes
- Checkers in Chinese
- The game of Clue
- Role-playing with masks or costumes
- Having fun with action figures
- Pretend tea parties
- Play therapy for older children
- Video games with strategy
- Video games for time management
- Superhero role-playing

- Art as a therapy

## The Science of Mind Games

Brain Teasers

Brain games have been shown by researchers from Kennesaw State University and Augusta State University in the United States to be a new form of ADHD therapy. Brain games help ADHD children overcome distractions by stimulating the prefrontal cortex of the brain. At the same time, such games could be used as an alternative to medication. According to the findings of the following tasks, brain games help develop the brain, improve focus and attention, and help ADHD children learn better. The current research is up-and-coming.

Following these findings, dozens of brain training programs arose, many of which made lofty claims not supported by science. My advice is to avoid these programs and instead focus on traditional brain games such as puzzles, riddles, and brain teasers. Don't give money to a phony program.

Brain games help children with ADHD by:

- Improving memory
- Developing problem-solving skills
- Improving logical thinking and deduction skills
- Improving concentration
- Promoting pattern recognition
- Video brain games that improve visual perception and spatial recognition
- Cognitive skill enhancement
- Reasoning skill enhancement

Coloring books have been around since our grandparents' time, but they are often overlooked in today's digital age. The advantages of coloring for your ADHD child, on the other hand, should not be ignored. Children are never too old to color, and paint has even been shown to help adults relieve stress! The advantages include:

- Preparing preschoolers for school
- Improving motor skills
- Developing good handwriting

- Enhancing creativity
- Developing color awareness
- Improving focus
- Improving hand-eye coordination
- Boosting confidence when children are praised for their work
- Improving self-expression abilities

The Sound of Music

While most activities engage either the left or right side of the brain, music engages both sides of the brain, improving your child's ability to multitask.

If your child has talent in music, encourage him by enrolling him in lessons, purchasing the instrument of his choice, or whatever else he requires to pursue his passion. Singing groups, orchestras, and choirs are also suitable places for your child to develop social skills and make new friends.

Theatrical

Drama groups and classes will be highly beneficial to your child if he enjoys acting and has the talent. He will have to concentrate on memorizing lines and learning to interact with others in a structured environment. To top it all off, the applause at the end of the show is what he needs in terms of praise and encouragement!

Debate Teams

That could be a delightful learning experience for your adolescent. It will hone their communication and social skills, stretch their intellect, and highlight their natural zeal and passion. It can also reduce stress and bring out their best qualities. Participate in a local, state, or the national debate team. Many debate programs are run and operated by students. They will have to follow the debate rules as a group. They are used to delivering directed speeches in front of large groups of people. They prepare lessons and distribute them. They are used to being creative, and their speech delivery and argument style are sometimes even artistic.

# Chapter 33:
# Emotional Development in Childhood

You don't have to get a psychology degree to be a good parent, not even when you are parenting a child with ADHD (or any other disorder). However, learning more about how your child will develop will help you create the right environment for them. Remember that parenting a child with ADHD can be significantly different than parenting other children, so knowing about their emotional development becomes even more important.

## From 0 to 12 Months

When children are born, they are often referred to as temperamental. They have strong, contradictory emotions and don't know how to deal with their feelings.

They express negative emotions more easily than positive ones, which makes them unpleasant to be around for anyone who doesn't want them as a friend. Because they have many of the same emotions as an adult, their expressions can be confusing—for example, when they are fussy and crying and no one knows why.

Babies also have a self-soothing mechanism, and they are at a phase where they are still learning a lot about the world (including how to differentiate facial expressions, for example). It is an age of marvel and discovery that borders on a miracle.

## From 12 Months to 2 Years

From the time your child is one to two years old, you will start to notice that they can recognize their emotions more easily. They've also developed the ability to regulate them and keep their impulses in check.

They're capable of seeing things from other people's perspectives without completely losing touch with their own point of view. This is true empathy: recognition of another person's feelings based on your own perspective, without losing yourself entirely.

## From 2 to 5 Years

The period from 2 to 5 is a time when children develop social skills. They will be able to read your moods and emotions and react accordingly.

They will start to develop self-control around the age of 4, but they will just have a conscious understanding of what this means and how it works.

Around the age of 5, children also start to develop a conscience — it is at this point that they start feeling guilty after doing something wrong.

## From 5 to 7 Years

The 5 to 7 years old period is one of the tremendous changes in terms of emotional development.

Your child will start to read their parents' facial expressions and emotions better, and they will start to learn how to make friends. They will understand the world better and be more able to consider other people's points of view.

They will also develop a greater sense of control over their impulses, which can help them avoid acting impulsively.

## From 7 to 10 Years

This is a period in which children develop their capacity to show sympathy to others. They will also be better able to consider others' perspectives and understand how their actions affect other people.

## From 10 to 13 Years

This is also a time of profound changes in emotional development. Your child will be more able to identify their feelings and recognize other people's feelings. They will have a deeper understanding of how their actions affect other people.

They will also be able to manage their emotions better. Parents should make sure that they understand the meaning of words like anxiety, stress, and depression so they can express themselves and get help when needed.

## From 13 Years Onwards

Your child will continue to develop into an adult, both emotionally and socially. They will have better emotional control and be able to make better decisions.

Though this period is often overlooked in families, it's an important one for your child's development (and how they will behave as adults later on in life). Although at this point your child might be more independent, it is important to acknowledge that they might still need your help (even if they don't specifically ask for it). As a parent, you will have to find the fine balance between offering to help and allowing your child to learn how to stand on their own feet.

Keep in mind that these stages of emotional development are quite standard, but that doesn't mean that all children follow the same patterns. In the case of a child with ADHD, it is important to help them build on what's normal for them. They may never be able to be as social as other children, but you can help them find balance and be as efficient as possible at acquiring friends and building steady relationships, for example.

You cannot expect things to happen to the textbook in the case of a child with ADHD. But you CAN expect them to eventually develop healthy emotions and ways of coping with their emotions from multiple points of view.

# Chapter 34:
## Discipline vs. Consequence vs. Punishment

Discipline techniques for other children might not work for explosive children, but there must be boundaries and codes of conduct established. That child needs a firm but loving hand when being corrected. You must fight to control your anger even when the child displays unacceptable behavior or is refusing to follow instructions. Removing privileges such as time playing computer games or looking at television is one way of dispensing discipline. Time outs are also a favorite for parents of those children. They should be put into effect as soon as the infringement is committed and should not last too long because the child won't complete it, and the effect will be lost. You also must be careful not to transfer your frustration at your child to your other children as they could end up being scolded a lot more severely than they deserved to be simply because you needed an outlet for your anger.

A sense of humor is precious in a home with an explosive child. You should learn to laugh instead of being embarrassed every time your child does things that might be socially unacceptable in a public place. It won't be easy but try to remember that the embarrassment will pass in time, and all that will be left would be a fun story to relate to your friends and relatives. Sometimes it is okay to ignore the unruly behavior if it is not causing anyone, including the child himself, any harm. That is not suggested as an ongoing way of dealing with tantrums and other misbehavior forms, but sometimes it is the right course of action. Those children need constant attention, and to get it, they would be willing to misbehave because negative attention is still attention. If your child is complaining and arguing for no reason, ignore him/her until it stops. If the complaining accelerates, let the child know that you would not be responding until he or she clams down. Like everything else, this will be successful sometimes but won't work in every instance. You will have to gauge when it is the right time to use it.

Your child is going to make many mistakes. Learn to compromise by letting the small ones pass. Pick your battles carefully and deal with issues individually. Don't try to solve every problem at once because that is setting yourself up for disappointment. Through all the challenges, never stop believing in your child and his/her ability to overcome. Make this clear to the child as well; he or she should always know that you believe in them. Stay positive. Encourage your child to vocalize their feelings. If he or she can tell you when he or she is feeling sad or angry, you might help them understand the problem before it leads to an episode of bad behavior.

Children with explosive disorder are expected to adhere to the family's rules just as other children do. However, because they are usually disorganized and impulsive, they need a structured existence even more than others. Make the rules clear to the child so they know precisely what is expected of them. Break down instructions into simple steps and speak in the most precise and most straightforward of ways. Look straight with your child's eyes when speaking to know that you have their attention. Have the child repeat what you said back to you. Many parents have found it helpful to engage in role-playing with their child to link them between their behavior and the reaction of the parent to it. Those children can often make that connection and establish it to help minimize unacceptable behavior.

These rules may need explaining a bit more often than with other children, so you must be patient but persistent and keep repeating the limits until they get it. Make the child understand that if the rules aren't followed, there will be consequences such as no television or spending time in their room, and if necessary, those consequences will be implemented.

## Positive and Negative Discipline Are Two Different Types of Discipline

Positive discipline inspires children to make better choices by guiding them toward more productive activities and praising them when they behave well, whereas negative discipline tends to involve sanctions and admonishing words to prevent them from acting badly.

With highly negative behaviors we must resort to punishment to mitigate or decrease them. Punishment should never be used alone, it goes along with the positive increase techniques described above. The use of punishment is reinforcing for the adult: it makes him feel the strongest, the outburst vents, immediately relieves tension... Its educational use, however, is more controversial than it may appear!

# How to Positively Discipline a Child

Before you lose your cool when your child misbehaves, realize that it is not their fault, nor yours. Discipline must be approached differently for explosive children.

Disciplining your children is unlikely to be among your top-five favorite aspects of parenting but keep in mind that you're not on your own. There's a lot of study on techniques you can use to make discipline simpler for you and your children. Read on to learn what works, what doesn't, and how to care for your nerves when they're stressed.

Parental Discipline Begins with Their Discipline

Children invariably respond to the parent's behavior. So be conscious of your stress levels and how they may affect your child. A good recommendation is for parents to conduct relaxation and deep breathing exercises for at least 10 seconds before talking to their children when stressed out.

Routine and Consistency Help to Prevent Outbursts Before They Occur

Routine and structure are incredibly crucial for children with explosive disorders. Here is how you can put it into action:

- Have regular schedules for school, homework, extracurricular activities, time with friends, and bedtimes. All are essential in helping children in remaining energetically and emotionally regulated to avoid at least some aggression from occurring.
- A well-balanced meal plan. Explosive disorders symptoms can be managed effectively with continuous exercise and a good meal-plan
- Get enough rest. Researchers discovered that low sleep quality and daytime sleepiness were linked to impaired executive functioning in children with explosive disorders.

Children's Timeouts Must Be Planned and Specified

To avoid confusion, you should make it obvious which actions are on the list. And when such behaviors occur, you can do the following:

Recognize and Reward Positive Behavior While Ignoring Unpleasant Outbursts

Children are subjected to a lot of criticism, and over time, they come to anticipate it. So rather than focusing on unpleasant outbursts, focusing on their positive behaviors will make your life and that of your child easier.

According to some researchers, given that every child reacts to things differently, rewarding positive actions might have the opposite impact, undermining child-rearing for some children and teenagers.

Therefore, it's important to pay attention to your child's response and take an unbiased look to see if they're learning the character behind the positive behavior or just doing what they have to do to get the reward.

Reward Only Those Who Deserve It

It's critical to be specific in your praise if you're going to employ a reward system. You don't have to claim your child did an excellent job just because they cleaned their room or didn't engage in undesirable conduct.

Instead, compliment them on the level of work they put into tidying their room. Also, avoid praising insignificant achievements or half-hearted attempts.

Children with an explosive disorder do have problems managing their behavior when rewards were inconsistent or the relationship between actions (their behavior) and a result (possible rewards) is unclear. To maximize the chances of getting the best results from them, parents should be consistent and clear in their rewards.

## What to Say and Must Never Say to Your Child

You may be at a loss for words if your child has recently been diagnosed with explosive disorders. Here's how you can communicate the situation to them, while also building them up.

Dos and Don'ts When Discussing Explosive Disorder with Your Child

- **Maintain an optimistic attitude:** When speaking with your child, this is the most vital thing to consider. If youngsters can see their disorder as a tool or something they can creatively utilize in the world rather than a barrier or problem to overcome, there are numerous potentials for personal growth.

You will have to embrace a growth mentality when dealing with your child. If a child can't accomplish something, it's because they can't do it yet; they can improve and work on it later.

With time, commitment and experience, instructors and parents can help their children organize their external environment by making it part of the child's education, so they can learn to handle it on their own.

- **Prepare them for success:** Explosion disorders do not imply that your child is incapable of focusing or completing tasks. If they are interested in anything, they can focus on it strongly, to the point that it is difficult to redirect their attention.

You can assist them in focusing by learning about their passions and creating a series of simple tasks that will demonstrate to them how well they can pay attention if they use their explosive disorders constructively.

What you could say: "explosive disorders don't define who you are," "There are many gifted people with explosive disorders. It just means you learn things uniquely and differently," "There is nothing wrong with you. Your brain just functions differently from that of others in that it works a bit faster and slowing it down can be difficult at times. But that's why, during class, we practice sitting still."

Don'ts When Discussing Explosive Disorders with Your Child

- **Do not chastise them:** Remember that even if your child appears to be deliberately pushing your buttons, they haven't been given the tools to handle their specific kind of explosive disorders. Your child isn't trying to irritate you on purpose all the time.

If your child's hyperactivity is pushing them to run about the house all the time, keep in mind that they aren't acting out of a want to be disruptive; rather, they are acting out of an impulse desire to move their body.

They'll start to better manage their urges and outbursts as they learn to grasp their explosive disorders and find better ways to control themselves (such as through a behavioral management plan).

It's also not a good idea to use a recent incident to start the conversation regarding their behavioral disorder. Because your emotions are likely to be heightened, it's preferable to have the conversation in a quiet, distraction-free environment.

- Don't make them feel bad about having explosive disorders: It is a regular observation from most parents and teachers to frequently tell explosive children that they are bad or dysfunctional. Spend less time focusing on what they're doing wrong and more time equipping them with knowledge of how unique and good they are.

Things to stay away from saying: "You're a child with a mental issue. That's just who you are," "Your life will be difficult, messy, and disorganized because of your problem," "You'll always struggle with learning things."

## The Cost of Response

Usually, gratifications are effective, but sometimes it is necessary to think of a point system, like stars or smiles, which allows for immediate gratification, but of course symbolic, that can then be converted into other types of rewards:

1. Define with the child the correct behaviors that will be rewarded.
2. Allocate points in proportion to the effort for the child (e.g., throwing the papers in the trash 1 point, doing all the homework 5 points).
3. Make a list with the child of things that are pleasant for him (e.g., a recess bonus, an assignment, a toy, a discount on an undesirable task), find the correspondence with the number of points.
4. Determine what causes you to lose points and how many points you lose (this is the cost of the answer).

5. Always respect the agreements for the exchange.

It may be helpful to make a chart sign, so progress is perceptible to the child and, why not, to the rest of the class.

Always accompany the administration of points with social rewards.

If we anticipate a fine in the form of an unwanted deprivation or activity, we must administer it without anger, directly and simply, and without further delay or explanation. Example: "You pulled Mary's hair, causing her to cry. You will lose ten minutes of break time by sitting in class alone. I don't want to hear any protests."

# Chapter 35:
# Parenting Principles

Keep in mind the several principles as you assist your child in developing ADHD strategies. These principles will assist you in guiding your child in a realistic and caring manner while keeping in mind that there is no cure-all for ADHD. Your guidance can help your child in understanding and dealing with the condition at their own pace.

## Practice Patience

Patience is a quality that all parents require, but it is significant for parents of children with ADHD. While it is natural for parents to solve their children's problems and "cure" their ADHD, most children require time to develop. According to NIMH and other studies, children with ADHD develop similarly to their peers, except for brain development, where they lag by about three years. According to these studies, parents can be confident that their children will eventually develop the necessary organizational, planning, and judgment skills demonstrated by children who do not have ADHD. However, the slower maturation path may necessitate more patience and a focus on long-term development rather than quick fixes.

## Keep an Eye on the Long Term

It has something to do with patience. Parents should be aware that they may not see immediate results while taking steps to assist their children. Change and maturation take time, and some children develop more slowly than others. They may face setbacks from time to time, but these hiccups in their development do not imply they will not eventually have all the tools they need for a rich and productive life.

## Ask Others for Help

Raising all children, especially those with learning differences truly does take a village. In other words, seek advice and support from a community of people who have children with ADHD, whether online or in your area. Enlisting the assistance of adults with whom your child interacts, such as teachers, coaches, tutors, doctors, therapists, and religious leaders, reflects positively on your parenting style. Enlisting the assistance of others may be especially important as your child approaches adolescence, a time when children are often less receptive to what their parents have to say.

## Externalize Rewards

Children with ADHD may not internalize motivation as other children do over time and they may require external reasons and supports to change their behavior. It does not imply that parents should bribe their children, but it does suggest that they should consider what children with ADHD value, such as playing video games or sports, and use these interests as rewards for children completing more mundane tasks. While many parents want their children to complete tasks simply because it is the right thing to do, children with ADHD may require external motivation until they develop a more intrinsic sense of what they need to do over time. External rewards are suggested in several strategies in this book to keep your child motivated.

## Recognize Positive Behaviors

Children with ADHD frequently require continuous feedback. Recognize what your child is doing well, even if it is only a tiny part of an immense task or something insignificant. For example, while most school-age children can dress and eat breakfast independently, many children with ADHD require praise for each step of the process to complete it on their own. Though many parents believe that they should not praise children for tasks expected of them at a certain age, children with ADHD require this praise to keep them motivated to complete these tasks independently. It may seem strange to praise children who are still developing skill sets that their peers have already incorporated—or that parents believe are simple—but it is necessary to keep ADHD children moving toward independence. Giant leaps can occur in unexpected time frames. Minor changes happen all the time; be unconditionally supportive of your child and notice when they succeed, no matter how insignificant the accomplishment may appear to you.

## Break Down Tasks and Directions into Smaller Parts

Must often break down tasks and directions into smaller, easier-to-manage chunks for children with ADHD. Avoid assuming that a child with ADHD will understand how to break down longer tasks on their own. For example, in the morning, your own child may require a list of all the tasks he must complete. As an example, consider the following:

1. Take your clothes from the drawer.
2. Put on your clothes, beginning with your socks, and so on.

School assignments must be divided in the same way. Additionally, specific completion times must be assigned, as many children with ADHD do not have an innate sense of how to plan or complete tasks within a particular frame of time.

## Communicate with Teachers and Other Professionals

Communicate openly and honestly with your child's teachers and other adults who interact with your child, such as camp counselors. Children with ADHD have a legal right to special school accommodations, such as an Individualized Education Program (IEP), to help them succeed. Many parents, however, try to conceal an ADHD diagnosis for fear of stigmatizing their child. Teachers and others in teaching and caregiving roles may assume a child is willfully defiant or disruptive if they are unaware of the diagnosis. If you communicate openly about your child's difficulties, teachers will be able to work with him or her more effectively. Parents should not request that their children be excused from assignments. Instead, they should consult with teachers about how to assist their children in completing their schoolwork.

## Avoid Comparing Children to Others, Including Siblings

It can be difficult for parents who have children with varying needs and developmental trajectories not to compare their children to their siblings or peers. Children with ADHD already have a powerful sense of not measuring up, and these types of comparisons do not tend to motivate them when shared with them. Making comparisons to show your ADHD child how they should behave can frustrate them even more and lead to a lack of self-confidence in working toward developing the skills they require.

## Keep in Mind the Particular Challenges of Girls with ADHD

While all children with ADHD may experience symptoms that interfere with positive social interactions, girls with ADHD may encounter cultural stereotypes about how they should act. For example, they may be regarded as odd, socially distractible, too terse, bossy, or possess other qualities that society, including many children, parents, and teachers, is not taught to value girls.

## Take Advantage of ADHD's Benefits and Energy

While ADHD does present challenges, it can also provide a great sense of creativity, high energy, and, in some cases, considerable charm. Parents should help their child explore to determine what they enjoy doing and encourage them to do it.

## Managing Impulsivity

Children with ADD/ADHD are impulsive and do not often consider their actions before acting. Although it might seem that they are deliberately defying you, they have trouble regulating their impulses. Tell your child to pause and think about doing something they know is wrong to help them learn to think before acting. Teach them to count to five or ten in their heads when taking deep breaths, depending on their age. It will help them feel better by bringing oxygen into the brain. After that, ask them, "What will happen if I do this?" Carry out the same procedure with your children. You teach them how to suppress their impulsivity, regain control over their body and mind through deep breathing, and consider the effects of their behavior.

## High Energy Levels

Much like managing impulsivity, children with ADD/ADHD tend to be impulsive and do not always think before acting. Teaching your child to think before they work tells them to stop and think about doing something they know is wrong. Again, teaching them to count to five or ten while taking deep breaths, increases the amount of oxygen in the brain, allowing them to think more clearly. Then make them realize what will happen if they do this—repeat this procedure with your child. You teach them to control their impulsiveness, regain control of their body and mind through deep breathing, and consider the consequences of their actions.

## Forgetfulness

While all children require reminders to bring their lunch to school and comb their hair, children with ADD/ADHD require more. They may intend to go upstairs to get their jacket, only to be distracted by the toys in their room. Understand that they are not attempting to annoy you but will simply require gentle reminders. If you've sent your child up for their jacket and they're taking too long, you can help them get back on track by saying, "Jacket," up the stairs. Visual aids may also help assist them in remembering. If they must always bring certain items to school, you could make a graphic to keep near their backpack. They must check that visual every day before they leave. You may have to remind them to avoid it, but that shifts some responsibility back to them.

## Focus and Concentration

While each child with ADD/ADHD will struggle to focus and concentrate, you can provide an environment that will assist them. Take the time to notice when your child is most alert during the day and when they may struggle. Perhaps specific triggers or transitions cause your child to become highly distracted. It could be when they first get home from school or when you do something out of the ordinary that isn't in the routine.

Once you've identified these times or triggers, plan your child's schoolwork around them so they can do it when they're at their best. It is also a good idea to create a distraction-free working environment, such as one free of toys, T.V., or video games. Working on homework or schoolwork with your child will also help them stay on track. Allowing your child to be active and move around the room will also help him or her concentrate or learn. If your child wiggles, have them sit on an exercise ball while doing their homework. They can be rocking and moving all the time while working.

These are just a few suggestions for working with a child with ADD/ADHD. Individualize these approaches based on your child's needs and what appears to work for your family. If you need help improving your child's ADHD behavioral management strategies, don't be afraid to seek professional help. Many specialists will visit the family's home and work with them on behavior management strategies. As you implement these strategies, you will notice positive changes in your child's behavior.

# Chapter 36:
# Time Management Tips

P lease don't take the tip categories too literally, or you'll miss some great ideas for your family. Good luck with your organization!

- Display a calendar or a stopwatch to your child. Instead of saying, "We're going to Grandma's house next week," say, "We're going to Grandma's in seven days," and each day, let your child cross a day off the calendar. Give your child their own calendar and let them own it. If you start this process early, your child will easily transition to a simple planner when he or she is ready for school.
- When requiring your child to share toys or take turns, use a timer, preferably one that allows you to see or hear the seconds pass. Because they are so focused on the present, your child needs to see time move.
- Before you leave the house to take your child to a fun place (where he is unlikely to want to leave), plan a routine for when to quit. It is best to go the same way whenever you visit a place where your child is unlikely to want to go. Habits serve as a child's emotional anchor, allowing him to transition more smoothly. Transitions are difficult for children in general. Assist them by anticipating changes before they occur.
- Provide your child with another enjoyable option when you require them to stop or leave a pleasurable activity. Encouraging them to leave the park cooperatively provides them with an enticing experience, such as an art and craft activity or a favorite treat. Always acknowledge and reward her cooperative behavior.
- Purchase a large clock timer that will sound when you enter the child's room to wake him up, relying on the clock rather than you.
- Post a household routine at your child's eye level so your child can learn how you structure his day. For your child, use broad visual cues. For young children, a pictorial schedule works well. Instead of writing breakfast, you could post a small image of toast and eggs or your child's favorite breakfast foods.
- Show your child how time is measured by having them retrieve an object or get something for you in the time allotted. You

could make it a game to see how quickly the child can get something for you, which has the added benefit of teaching the child how to clean up quickly.
- Set aside a time for the whole family to clean the house and let your toddler or preschooler clean while keeping an eye on the timer. When you assign him an unpleasant task, this works incredibly well. The child begins to understand that time is not related to the difficulty of a chore but instead to its duration.
- Give your children incentives if they notice a schedule change and cooperate with you. While young children require structure, they must also accept that it will disrupt their schedule at times. They must accept that fact graciously. It promotes respect for time and design while also developing healthy coping skills.
- Young ADHD children are just coming into their own, and they need to understand that time is an entity in and of itself. If you can get them to grasp this concept, they will be well on their way to mastering time. Engage them in a conversation using time words such as after, never, and so on.

## 6 to 9 Years Old in School

- Post calendars in children's rooms, particularly for early elementary school children. With little time they become the child's personal property to cross off the days until a specific event occurs.
- Have your children make or decorate calendars every month. Purchase blank calendars from websites or create your own. Check out our list of resources.
- Purchase an organizer/planner for your child and demonstrate how to use it. Many children already own planners but are unsure how to use them. The planners must be simple to use. They must be checked regularly until recording in the planner becomes a routine or habit for her. For young children, the planner should be broad-ruled, with a month-at-a-glance view and the ability to use their assignments weekly rather than daily. When children only document things every day, they do not develop considerable picture thinking skills. They will also require practice in which you think it with them until it becomes second nature.
- Make it a habit to remind your children that time is measured in seconds, minutes, and hours. Jumping jacks (or arm flaps or

another equivalent physical action) should be done for one second, one minute, and five minutes. Discuss how you felt after doing the same thing for the specified amount of time.
- Set fun writing or drawing assignments for your child (this only works if she enjoys drawing or writing). Call time when you notice the child is engrossed in the activity. When you call time after only about fifteen minutes, your child will become irritated.
- In general, we focus on intervals of fifteen minutes or less. Young children will begin to understand the importance of planning their projects in a short amount of time.
- Set the timer regularly to give your child a set amount of time to complete a creative task or do something around the house. If your child shows signs of frustration and does not begin working on the project, talk about what he would have done and have him repeat the task frequently. As it occupies your child, this activity is also great for giving mom or dad some much-needed quiet time by using this as a springboard to discuss the importance of realistically planning study times.
- Display a household routine in an appropriate location so your child can begin to understand how you plan his day. Use big visual cues for your child and include his school schedule in your planner, so he understands the connection between home and school planning.
- Provide your children with a clock and a non-negotiable bedtime. That is a fantastic opportunity for your child to start standing up for himself and understanding. Along with the privilege of getting up on his own comes the responsibility of going to bed early.
- Use a family calendar to keep track of important dates and events. As a result, the child begins to understand that the entire family operates within time constraints.
- Talk about setting a goal with your child. Choose a fun destination, such as learning to skateboard, and then allow your child to write down everything that needs to be done to reach the goal.
- Please encourage your children to set educational goals in the same way they would set fun goals, such as riding a skateboard. The child learns to anticipate, plan, and set goals, which can apply to almost any situation.

- Invest in a family timer. Every evening, place this timer in the center of the family dinner table. At the end of each day, instruct the child to set the timer for 12 minutes that they can answer questions, make a to-do list of tasks for the next day, or enjoy quiet family time. Make sure that the child notices you using the timer every evening.
- Use a flow chart, similar to a drawn racetrack, to help your child visually track his progress through a task. I once used a racetrack to demonstrate to young children that they were making progress toward their reading goals. They moved the car forward with each step they took toward their reading goals.

## Tweens Aged 9 to 12

- Hang calendars with hobbies or interests in your tween's room. Because the calendars contain your child's interests, they will use anything they can empathize with personally.
- Assign a summer study project or conduct family research. It should be enjoyable while requiring little research. Show your child how to complete the project by using the time grid and study plan.
- Inspire your child to make a to-do list for any special projects. Request that they estimate the amount of time it will take to complete each task. You can accomplish this by simply taking a large piece of paper and writing down the top three tasks they need to do to complete the project. Keep an eye on everything, and then have your child arrange them chronologically.
- Designate a child to be the family organizer for the week. This child can ensure that the entire family follows the rules of order and organization. She might, for example, check to see if everyone is doing their chores. That's an excellent job for a middle child, who doesn't often get to take the lead or have a say in family decisions. Many families will accept the family baby or listen to a dominant oldest child, but this allows a middle child to shine.
- Rotate the role of family time and organization manager between siblings or between you and your child every week. The family time manager oversees updating the family calendar and reminding everyone about upcoming appointments. We learn best by doing; giving your child the responsibility of monitoring his/her time will do wonders for her self-esteem.

- Assign your child the task of completing a project, such as cooking a portion of the holiday meal. Show your child how to break the job down into sequential steps and how much time each step takes. You are teaching timed stages to progress goal setting.
- Ask your child what they want to do when they grows up, and then have them research how to get there. It will also help if they know you will collaborate with to achieve their objectives.
- Please encourage your child to record personal and school activities in a planner to learn how time management affects both personal and school life.
- As a child, read a biography of a famous person. Encourage your child to notice how the person exhibited successful traits even as a child. It provides them with a vision for their future.

# Chapter 37:
# Life Skills Your Child Needs to Master

Studies show that ADHD persists in adolescence in 50 to 80% of the cases, and in adulthood in 35-65% of the cases (CHADD, 2021). Those might look like exceedingly high numbers, but the reality is that the right treatments and management systems can lower the odds that your child ends up having severe issues well into their teenage and adult years.

In essence, together with your child and your child's therapist, you should focus on helping the little one develop essential life skills that will help them perform better. Every parent needs to do this with their child, regardless of whether they have ADHD. However, in the case of ADHD children, the symptoms might make it a little more challenging (but not impossible!).

Here are some life skills your ADHD child will have to master:

## Independence

All children need to be taught how to do things independently and, over time, to become self-sufficient. Let me illustrate this with an example:

If a child likes playing video games and you allow them to play for hours on end, then they won't learn how to make their own meals, do their own laundry, plan their own social schedules, etc. They will simply remain dependent on you for every little thing!

If your ADHD child is having trouble listening or following simple instructions at home (e.g., doing the dishes, taking out the garbage, or doing homework), then it would be a good idea to sit down with them and teach them how to do these simple tasks.

## Social Skills

ADHD children tend to experience difficulties when it comes to social skills. This might be because of the way they look at things or they might simply not know how to talk properly. With the right approach and treatments, however, children with ADHD can learn how to properly socialize, make friends, and grow relationships with other people.

## Time Management

Most children with ADHD have a hard time with it but the key is to teach them that they have to make a schedule and stick to it. They will need their own planner or diary for this to be possible, as well as different tools to make effective use of it. It is not at all impossible for a child with ADHD to develop good time management skills, especially if they are taught how to organize their time from a very young age.

## Organization

Another thing that ADHD children struggle with within their lives is organization. There are times when a child will be able to engage in both hyperactive and impulsive behavior and other times when they will be quite calm and organized. Therefore, it would be good for parents to teach their children about the value of the organization as early as possible.

This way, the child will know what it means to have a well-ordered life and will also learn how to keep everything neat and tidy, both in their physical surroundings, and when it comes to how they organize their thoughts.

## Money Management

Many people with ADHD are great at getting into trouble when it comes to money, lying, stealing, or any other type of crime that involves money. An ADHD child will need to learn how to control their impulses and focus on achieving realistic goals. For this to happen, parents should teach their children about budgeting, planning, and saving money.

## Taking Medications

Many children with ADHD do very well with medication. However, this is not an easy road to navigate since they can develop side effects and require adjustments in the dosage as they grow older. Therefore, your child must take his or her medications regularly and appropriately (and that they learn the importance of doing so).

## Relationships

Some adult cases of ADHD maintain the same behavior as they did when they were children. However, it does make sense to teach them how to build and maintain relationships with other people.

For them to build and maintain relationships, children with ADHD should learn how to pay attention in class, develop friendships, and organize their day around meeting other people in social situations.

## Anger Management

Children with ADHD tend to be very emotional and angry, so it is important for you as a parent to teach them how to handle these emotions and how to make sure they do not affect them (or others around them).

## Wise Decision-Making

Though ADHD children might be very impulsive and quick to react, they do not necessarily make the best decisions, to begin with. They can learn how to make better decisions by learning from their mistakes and watching others who are successful in similar situations.

The more they learn about the consequences of their actions the more likely it is that they will make better decisions in the future.

An ADHD diagnosis does not have to mean your child cannot grow into a successful, functional, and independent adult. It takes time to get there, and it takes effort on all ends. It is more than doable, especially with the knowledge we now have of this disorder.

# Chapter 38:
# Build Your Child's Self-Esteem

One of the main sources of explosive child's self-esteem is the haters in the society who don't know anything about the disorder and treat it as an untouchable thing. The reason behind this is the several misconceptions that are present in society.

Very often, you will find that skeptics make it clear that adults cannot have ADHD and that they are simply using it as an excuse to cover up their faults. They keep saying that whatever symptoms they have or claim to have are because their parents did not rein them in when they were young. They will tell you to deal with your shortcomings and grow up. But I have already given you plenty of evidence in this book to support the fact that explosive disorders are real. It is very real, and it happens in adults as well. So, if you do have to reply to the skeptics, do so with facts. The best ammunition you have against the skeptics of society is hard facts. You can even take them to one of your meetings with your support group or send them articles that will educate them.

But if you are looking for something sarcastic, you can always tell them how nice it is for them to be smarter than some of the most renowned psychologists and scientists in the world.

Then comes another group of people who are best described as the crusaders. They will question every step you take and every decision you make. They will second-guess your choice of doctor or even your medication. They might even tell you that explosive disorders medications are nothing but "kiddie cocaine." You must present them with facts that, like every other medication, explosive disorders meds have their side effects too. But that does not mean they are going to inculcate a feeling of dependency in the patient.

Before you go spouting off things to others, you need to make sure you have your facts straight.

Parents, relatives, and other authority figures, such as teachers and caretakers, may lose patience with the explosive child or the child with ADD/ADHD, become upset, and attempt to criticize and correct their conduct. Since there is much negative feedback coming from various sources, they internalize it and start to feel awful about themselves.

According to several studies, when children with explosive disorders mature into adults, their self-esteem continues to erode over time due to increasing criticism and complex life events.

## Children's Self-Esteem

Growing up with explosive disorders can cause self-esteem issues, making it difficult to take acceptable risks in relationships and friendships, careers, education, and the workplace. Without taking those chances, further progress may be restricted or nonexistent.

When a person has strong self-esteem, they feel good about themselves and regard themself as deserving of others' respect. When a person you has poor self-esteem, they do not respect their own thoughts and opinions. They are concerned that they are not good enough most of the time.

Rather than viewing an explosive disorder as a personal fault, we must help others to enhance their self-esteem by concentrating on learning strategies to be successful with their symptoms. With younger children, one should typically avoid using the term explosive disorder, leaving it up to their parents. Instead, it challenges students to produce a term for the brain type they possess. Call it 'attention-wandering brain' or 'quick brain' in the workplace. Maybe you have a 'many ideas brain.'

While teenagers may feel relieved, many are still concerned that explosive disorders may separate them from their peers or hinder them from reaching their objectives. We must assist children in identifying role models with an explosive disorder, such as Michael Phelps or Simone Biles. The aim is always to accept the brain that you have.

For every harmful statement, children need to receive three nice or encouraging ones. An informal survey to see how many negative remarks a child or teen hears in comparison to good comments. According to estimation, for every 15 negative remarks, a child with an explosive disorder receives just one good comment. They internalize the negativity, which affects a person's self-assurance.

Parents can do much to help their children overcome their low self-esteem. Refer to the method as the 5 Cs of parenting:

- **Self-control:** First and foremost, learn to regulate your own emotions so you can behave successfully and teach your children to do the same.
- **Compassion:** Accept your child for who they are, not who you think they should be.
- **Collaboration:** Instead of forcing your rules on the child and co-parent, work together to discover answers to daily difficulties.
- **Consistency:** Maintain consistency by doing what you say you will do again and over again.
- **Celebration:** Recognize what works and do more of it day after day.

Celebration is truly noticing, and it is recognizing and validating the good developments you observe. You may boost a child's self-esteem by recognizing and validating both their accomplishments and efforts. You are fostering their tenacity and self-assurance.

When an explosive disorder diagnosis is made, it should provide a chance to analyze the past better and then put in place the behavioral and academic assistance that will help in the future. Providing opportunities for achievement can allow a child or teen's self-esteem to be rebuilt and strengthened.

"Learning how to do this and skills, as well as the emotions of coping with it," is one of the essential things after an explosive disorder diagnosis.

How can you identify if your child is having issues with his or her self-esteem?

A huge indication is that they regularly make critical comments about one, even after small mistakes. They may refuse to try something new, even though they have in the past. This might indicate that they do not believe they are competent or talented enough to thrive in new hobbies.

They may say things like, "Well, I am not a great student, then why should I try any longer?"

They may also ignore or minimize some possibilities, claiming, "It is dumb anyhow," since they are unsure of their capacity to thrive. Furthermore, they could be gloomy about alternative possibilities.

They may distance from friends or family, lose interest in things they formerly enjoyed, experience an increased or reduced appetite (not related to developmental changes such as growth spurts or puberty), receive poorer grades, or lose friends.

## Different Ways to Safeguard a Child's Self Esteem

Praise your child for accomplishments while also acknowledging and mentioning the obstacles that made it difficult for your child to do so. Regular negative criticism might damage your child's self-esteem. Recognize your child's accomplishments, no matter how minor they may be. Try to observe when your child is paying attention or doing what he is meant to be doing—and what discipline and skills he used to get there.

Tell your child what they did well—not just a generic "good work!" but something specific like "I love how you thought about the task and organized your outline!" This will not only boost your child's self-esteem but will also reinforce his grasp of what it takes to thrive so he can repeat the process. This can also educate him to appreciate small victories instead of being overly harsh on himself.

Describe any mental or emotional obstacles he had to face to get ahead in this situation. Just an example that, "You understand that other ideas sidetracked him, but he or she fought hard to overcome them and stay on track. "Congratulations!"

Explosive disorders frequently give mirror characteristics that are valuable. Recognize your child's assets. They may not be a great reader, but has the potential to be the next Picasso. They might not be great at writing reports, but have an uncanny ability to come up with innovative ideas. Recognize, reward, and capitalize on your child's skills so that he or she feels proud and accomplished.

Recognize that they may be experiencing lingering anxiousness after school and that he requires time to wind down by doing something he enjoys. Make that dynamic explicit so that they learn to understand their own emotions and how to cope with and conquer them.

Ascertain that your child has the potential to thrive while participating in these hobbies and that untreated disorder explosion does not harm their abilities. Also, do not ruin the enjoyment by depriving them of activities they enjoy as a prize for performing the ones they dislikes.

Setting and accomplishing objectives, big and little, makes children feel powerful. Encourage your child to develop a list of things they want to do to help them transform their ambitions and dreams into practical objectives. After that, practice breaking down relatively long goals into manageable milestones. You validate their passions and assist them in developing the abilities they will need to achieve their life objectives.

Break down difficult jobs into tiny incremental steps or components to assist your youngster in completing them. Recognize their successes at each stage; this will boost their confidence, motivate them to take the next step and teach them how to break down projects into manageable sub-tasks—and organizing skills.

Many youngsters may use their rooms as "horizontal storage" for their toys, covering each inch of the floor. Sit down with your youngster and walk him through each category of cleaning one at a time. "Where are all the red trucks going?" "Great! Where are all the blue vehicles going now?" "I loved how you painstakingly sorted the toys into categories—now you will know where it all belongs!" say once it is all done.

Be available for your child every day. A special occasion, whether it is an outing, playing games, or simply spending time with your child in good interaction, may assist in strengthening your child's self-worth. It also promotes healthy attachment; studies have shown that insecure connection is linked to explosive disorders and impedes the development of a good self-image.

With your youngster, practice social skills. Because of their hyperactive, impulsive, or violent actions, children with explosive disorders may be shunned by their classmates. Play role-playing games with your youngster in a variety of social situations. Ask them to imagine how a friend, for example, might react if they did certain things or acted in a certain manner. Request that your youngster act it out. Then urge them to envision an alternate way of acting that would not anger or irritate their friend. Choose one-word codes or signals to indicate each desired action. Invite one of their peers over for a supervised play session and call out the applicable code words as needed to encourage your child to choose the more successful action they demonstrated.

Recognize such moments and give yourself permission to take a deep breath and consider how your child is feeling. This is when it is even more critical that you recognize and show your love for your child's ongoing challenges. Let your child know that you'll be there for them through both good and bad times.

## Protecting Their Self-Esteem While Helping Them Grow

There is another extremely important part of training explosive children, and that is encouragement. After all, your goal is not to just get them to master a task but to get them to feel good about mastering it. One of the most damaging parts of anyone's psychological state is when words are used in the wrong way.

Some parents, out of frustration will use force, ultimatums, and punishments to intimidate the child into better behavior. These types of actions are often based on the idea that the child is being deliberately rebellious and willful.

As we've already learned, this is not the case with explosive children. While punishment may be warranted from time to time, it is not the most effective way to teach. The focus is on the bad behavior and not the positive. It doesn't address the issue of teaching the child correct behavior but instead concentrates on teaching them what not to do. Add to that the fact that harsh words are painful; when they come from the person they rely on to help them through life, it is especially difficult to hear. In time, it drives a wedge between you, one that will continue growing to separate you more each time they are shared. Eventually, you could find yourself separated from your child by a deep chasm that may be nearly impossible to overcome.

The best solution, therefore, is to use positive praise and encouragement to guide your child in the right direction. Praise given can do wonders for your child's self-esteem if done correctly. The easy way is to say words like, "good job," "that's awesome," or "I'm so proud of you." These are wonderful ways to start a positive dialogue with your child. However, studies have shown that when you are more specific, the praise yields the best results. Instead of "good job," try something like, "I like the way you came in and started your homework right away, good job!" Now the child knows exactly what they are being praised for.

Even when you give praise, you must be careful how you do it. Maybe you've seen those parents who mix praise and criticism. "You did a good job washing the dishes, why can't you do that all the time?" This kind of praise often confuses and frustrates the child rather than reinforces the spirit. At best, it reduces the power that your positive words are trying to say. Next are a few basic guidelines that can teach you how to give appropriate praise to your child when needed.

## Teach Yourself to Pay Positive Attention

Parents are often busy with affairs and forget to set aside one on one time with their children. Try to block out a time when it is just you and the child and observe them. Don't hover over them like a mother hen but let them move about freely in their activity and watch what they are doing. If they are playing a game, don't jump in right at the beginning but sit back and watch for a while. Once you understand what they are doing narrate their actions back to the child, so they understand. This works better when you show a little enthusiasm in your descriptions. Match your enthusiasm to the age of the child. Younger children enjoy more animation, but you can tone it down as they get older.

As you speak, give them both verbal and non-verbal signs of approval when you see them doing something you like.

Non-verbal signs could include a hug, wrapping your arm around them, a pat on the head, a soft rub on the shoulder, a high-five, a smile, or a wink. Verbal skills could mean saying things like "I like it when you do..." Or "that is so grown up when you do..."

You can also praise progress. "Last year you couldn't do...but now look at you."

If during your time together, the child misbehaves, turn your attention away and focus on something else. That usually works to get the child to adjust their conduct. If the bad behavior persists, tell them that your time together is over and that you'll spend time again when they can control their behavior.

## Be Clear in Your Commands

When giving a command to your child, the compliance begins with you. Never give a command that you do not genuinely expect them to do. Back up every request with the reward or consequences outlined.

Do not make it in the form of a question as this can give them the idea that obedience is optional. Do not say, "why don't you get ready for bed now?" rather make it direct, "get ready for bed." When you raise your inflection at the end of the sentence, children will subconsciously believe that you are asking them if they want to get ready for bed. Make sure your tone is clear enough to let them know you expect compliance.

## Teach Your Child Not to Interrupt

Children crave attention and will do anything to get it. If you give a lot of attention to a child that interrupts, you can expect to continue to have a parade of interruptions. To avoid this problem, before you are engaged in any type of activity like talking to a neighbor or on the phone give them a command to do something that will keep them occupied while you are otherwise engaged.

Make sure that the task you ask them to do is something they will enjoy. If the child obeys your instructions, stop what you're doing for a second to give them praise. As the child becomes accustomed to this type of instruction and praise, you can extend the time between praises to keep them engaged.

If they look as if they're going to interrupt you, stop and give them praise for obeying what they're doing and then refocus their attention on the task you want them to do.

In the end, make sure you praise or reward the child for following your instructions before you go on to another activity.

## Use Constructive Punishment

When children become defiant or disobey, it is important to remember that it is not that they are refusing to follow your commands. Outright defiance is not a characteristic of explosive disorders. What is happening is that their lack of executive skills often pulls them away mentally from whatever task you've assigned. It could be that the task is very boring or very hard, which can be very uncomfortable for them.

Punishment, however, should be used as a last resort. It is better to find a more positive and self-edifying means of praise and incentives to motivate the child. There are several ways to punish a child in a way that helps them get the point.

Fines: If you used the reward system to motivate them you could also use the fine system to remove privileges. For example, if they receive 5 tokens for obeying your directives you can choose to deduct tokens for disobedience.

## Manage Your Child in Public Places

The secret to getting your child to be obedient in public lies in the preparation. Make sure they know what's expected of them before you go out. Give them a brief list of rules to follow and make sure they understand them. Have them repeat them back to you, so they own the instructions. Review the instructions before you go in and if they disobey take them out to your car and wait until they are ready to try again.

Establish an incentive to motivate them to obey your directives and punishment if they disobey.

Keep them busy. Give them an activity that they enjoy keeping them occupied. It is good to have several ready to go so you can keep them engaged while you are out.

No matter which methods you use to manage your child's behavior whether in public or at home, they should be used consistently so as not to confuse the child. It will not be an easy ride, but if you are consistent, there is real hope that in the end your child will respond and grow from the experience. While it is easier said than done, never take a child's behavior personally or to the point that you forget you're working with a child with a disability. Learn the art of forgiveness for both your child and for yourself, and you'll both be happy about it.

# How to Help Explosive disorders Children Make Friends

Building Friendship Growth Opportunities

For elementary and preschool children, playdates offer a great opportunity for parents to model and coach positive peer interactions for them. For the child, they will be able to practice these new skills. You can set up these playtimes with one or two friends at a time—keep it minimal rather than having a large group of friends as this may be overwhelming for the child and you. Plan playtime to be the most effective for your child.

Consider yourself as your child's friendship mentor. Consider carefully how long a playdate takes and select activities that are most interesting for your child.

The older the child gets, friendships and peer relationships become more complicated but continue to remain involved in your child's life and help them facilitate interactions that are positive for themselves. For a child who struggles socially, middle- and high school years can be harsh. It would be good if the child can have a least one or two good friends throughout the years of school that can often be the child's support system rather than having a large group of friends.

Socially alienated middle- or secondary school students who face constant rejection may feel desperate to become members of any peer group, including those with adverse impact.

Another way to foster positive peer relationships outside of school is to get involved in groups within the community such as Indian Guides, Boy Scouts, Girl Scouts, Girls Who Code, Rotary Club for children, sports teams, and art groups. When your children join these clubs and teams, ensure that group leaders or mentors know about explosive disorder and create an environment that is both encouraging and constructive for your child. This is extremely helpful overall.

Don't be worried or afraid to share information about your child's condition with kindergarten, coaches, and parents in the community so you know what's going on with your child and who's spending time with your child. Withholding information will only make things worse. The peer group of a child and the features of the group affect the individuals in the group strongly.

Empowering the Peer Status of Your Child through School

Peer groups are important for children, but the downside is that once they put a label on your child because of their lack of social skills, it can be hard to break away from this reputation. Having a reputation, especially one that isn't *cool*, can become an obstacle for your child. Negative peer labels are commonly established when the child is in early to middle school and this reputation does not fade away easily, even though the child develops positive social skills. This is one of the main reasons why it is extremely crucial for parents to collaborate with the school and their child's teachers, mentors, and coaches to address any effects.

Lessening or stopping these negative impacts can be done through establishing a positive working relationship with your child. Inform them about the strengths and desires of your child as well as what they struggle with. You can also share any approaches that you find helpful in focusing on the areas of weakness of your child.

When forming social preferences about their peers, young children often look to their teacher. A teacher's presence, warmth, acceptance, patience, and gentle direction can be an excellent model for the peer group, and it also influences the child's social status. The teacher plays a significant role in finding other ways to draw positive attention to the explosive disorder child.

This gives opportunities for the peer group to view the child in a positive and encouraging light, which also helps to stop the group process of peer rejection. It can help to promote social acceptance by pairing the child with a caring friend in the classroom.

Setting Up Accommodations in School and at Home

The benefits of having a good, working relationship with your child's teacher are enabling them or helping the teacher outfit explosive disorder techniques and methods in the classroom. This helps the child to manage their symptoms better. Working together with a teacher or an adult caregiver, therapist, or coach on effective approaches towards behavior management and social skills is the best and most practical solution.

Inform your child's teacher about the medication your child takes, especially if they need to take it during school hours. Be sure to work closely with the child's doctor as well because you may need to give feedback on your child's responses and symptoms, both at home and school. With this information, the doctor can fine-tune and adjust the child's medication along the way.

# Chapter 39:
# Help Children Manage Anxiety During the Pandemic

As the pandemic progresses, more parents are becoming concerned about how their children are responding to the ever-changing news. Some children will be no less anxious than they were before, while others may respond by suddenly feeling much better or worse. There is a great deal of the usual variability in how children react to the pandemic news. And there may also be a wide range in how the children feel and/or behave after the news, even within the same family.

Many parents are asking for advice on how to help their children cope with the imminent pandemic. Several books have been written about how to manage anxieties during a crisis. The problem is that not all situations are alike, and not all people respond uniformly to any situation. Most of these books also reflect a scientific model of how children react to the news.

## Combatting Anxiety in Your Children

It is good to start with the basics and take it up from there. This means ensuring that you and your children are exposed to the basics of care. These include:

Getting the Right Amount of Sleep

No matter what, you should never meddle with sleep time. Your children need the right amount of sleep to aid their emotional wellbeing and help their brain function optimally. This is not for children and adolescents only but includes people of all ages. You know how you feel when you're running on little to no sleep. You are exhausted, irritable, and unable to stay alert as usual while increasing the risks of exhibiting depressive symptoms. Now, that's for you, the adult. So, imagine how your children will react to a lack of sleep mixed in with anxiety. This will only affect the important physiological processes necessary for their maturation. Activate the right sleep hygiene measures, which will ensure optimal sleep. These include:

- Exposing your children to as much natural light as possible during the day.
- Eliminating spicy or fatty foods just before bedtime.
- No caffeinated drinks.
- No screens emitting blue light, including TV, laptops, or smartphones, an hour before bedtime.
- Use the perfect room temperature.
- Stick to a regular bedtime schedule.
- For parents, you should make sure that you have no coffee or other caffeinated drinks late in the evening. When I say attend to the basics, you are not left out too.
- Implement the precautions.
- Note for any sign of illness in your children.

Exercise

Engage in regular physical activity with your children. This shouldn't be anything too complicated but age-appropriate enough to maintain their physical wellness.

## Don't Be Afraid to Seek Professional Help

If you ever have a reason to believe at some point that your child has a mental health condition, it is okay to seek professional help. There are many helplines available with professionals who can guide you on the right steps to take. You may miss the symptoms of childhood anxiety at first because you erroneously thought that they would outgrow the "bizarre" behavior. However, as you realize that this is anxiety, it is important that you don't believe that this should be left to you alone. It is okay to get some psychological support as well as you need to be at optimal mental health to offer the needed guidance and support for your children with anxiety.

## Attending to the Basics

Here are tips that will help you bring some semblance of normalcy in your home as you try to calm the anxiety in your children:

Provide Some Structure to the Day

There is so much unpredictability in these times, and your day shouldn't be too. A day with no clear schedule can contribute to the high level of anxiety in your home among your children and teens. Help your children feel some sense of accomplishment by having a definite daily schedule. For parents working from home, you can do this in such a way that it doesn't encroach on your work time. Be sure not to go overboard with the scheduling, as it is beneficial to do this in moderation. When it's too restrictive, you could be sitting on a time bomb as well. Be flexible with the schedule but keep the wake-up time and bedtime as regular as possible.

Pick Your Battles

While this may be from a place of love, a lot of parents give in to the urge to correct every single move of their child that they consider annoying. At this point, you will have to pick your battles and focus more on positive feedback. Since these children will be home with you for more hours than usual, this will only amplify negative feelings in your home. So, try to disengage from this action. Instead of picking out every single time they mess up or are annoying, you should praise their desirable behavior. This shouldn't be general, but more specific to show that you are paying attention.

You need to be able to tell the difference between an annoying behavior and a dangerous one. The annoying behavior may just be your child trying to cope with the situation in the way they know how to and could be completely unintentional. You will only reinforce the undesirable behavior when you pay more attention to it. Negative criticism and feedback shouldn't be too constant, as it will only ruin your child's self-esteem.

Prioritize Spending Quality Time Together

Your schedule should include activities you can participate in with your children. Even as little as twenty minutes of quality time spent with your children regularly will go a long way. These children will feel calmer, understood, and supported as they see how much you're willing to go to create time for them. Your activities should be age-appropriate. For example, those below ten years of age would put a different meaning to quality time compared to those above that age range. You can use free-play or child-directed play for the younger age group. This simply means letting the child be in charge of the direction of the play rather than giving instructions or telling him/her exactly what to do.

Practice Mindfulness

This is more for you than for your children. It's okay to take a few minutes to pause and slow down. You can do this through mindful pauses during the day. This will aid both you and your child with a progressed passionate wellbeing level, as you'll be able to recapture point of view amid those overpowering times.

You're more likely not to overreact when you're already in a state of calm. With mindfulness, you can be more effective at practicing better parenting during the pandemic by being less reactive and more patient.

Let Your Children Take up Hobbies

Now is a good time to put hobbies on the schedule. While schoolwork is important, you shouldn't neglect the creative part of your children that is necessary for their developing brain. It could be literally anything that you know would add value to their lives and help them find some purpose during this pandemic. There is a lot of free time now anyway, so no excuses. You could encourage them to get started on activities such as reading, painting, drawing, writing, dancing, singing, or playing a musical instrument. Now that you are home with them, you can encourage your children to explore their creativity. This will give them a sense of joy and fulfillment, which is important for their cognitive and emotional wellbeing in the long run.

Limit the Use of Media

You don't have to monitor actively the number of coronavirus cases and deaths every day. This is not only bad for your children but could put a severe dent in your mental health as well. As you expose them to that horrible news, it could be confusing, scary, and exhausting for your children.

While it's okay to stay up-to-date on happenings around you, this should be limited to as little as possible based on the developmental level and age of your children. You will realize that the household feels calmer when you're not watching every day as people lose their lives. This should not be confused with shielding them from what's going on.

They deserve to know without being kept in the dark. When explaining to them what is happening on the news, be as f as possible.

Keep Them Connected with Friends

One of the hallmarks of the novel coronavirus is that we are unable to physically meet with friends and family. This social isolation could be disastrous for children, as they must get used to the fact that they can't leave home as much as they want. They can't hug their friends or engage in those activities they most likely took for granted. You can follow the guidelines stipulated by the CDC by taking advantage of the technology at your fingertips. Organize video chat sessions where they can connect with their friends using their social media accounts, smartphones, or laptops. The teens will most likely have social media accounts, and you can supervise this minimally to ensure that they are using it appropriately.

Engage Them in Developmentally Appropriate Tasks

Let them do things for themselves in situations where you know they can handle it. You can entrust them with the tasks of cleaning up paint after painting, putting their crayons back, folding laundry, or rolling out the dough. These are all developmentally appropriate tasks that will help them gain confidence, agency, and a sense of mastery. You can also get them in on the simple household activity. For teenagers, you can encourage them to help their younger siblings with their learning activities. They can also help you shop online for groceries and other essentials. Remember to supervise and monitor these tasks to avoid putting your child in harm's way.

Stay Calm, Listen, and Offer Reassurance

You are your child's role model, and they will be actively learning from the example you set. Be sure to react as calmly as possible to situations as your children will respond to your reactions. So, how do you talk about COVID-19 when you think they are not listening? Save the serious conversations for when you're sure they are not lurking around. You don't want to increase your children's fear unnecessarily. You also don't want to decrease it in such a way that they have no regard for their personal safety.

Be sure to remind your children that you are all healthy and reassure them that you will continue to ensure that they are all safe and well during the pandemic. This is also a good time to encourage them to write out their feelings while you respond as truthfully as possible.

Encourage Them to Help Others

This is a good time to take them on a lesson in empathy. You can identify projects that will help others around you and encourage your children to participate. These can be tasks as little as writing letters to your neighbors that are stuck at home alone. You can even encourage them to send messages of hope to healthcare workers or other positive messages on social media. Just as you're feeling a little blue with the current situation, your children can talk with others and draw strength from each other.

# Chapter 40:
# Support Your Child During the Pandemic

All of us have been affected by what is happening in the world right now. There are many questions, especially for parents. Worries about how to protect your child from this or that or which emergency kit to buy.

Here we'll be talking about how to support your child during this pandemic and the steps you can take to keep your family safe.

First, you need to know that there is no vaccine or medication to prevent the flu, so the best thing you can do is take preventive measures. Have your children wash their hands more often and when in public avoid getting close to people with a cough or sneeze. (Use a tissue when needed, dispose of it properly, and wash your hands).

Your child might fear what's happening right now, so try to ease their worried mind. Watch the news with them, answer their questions, and make them understand not only adults who get sick.

If your child has and already been exposed to the virus, don't panic. They are probably feeling tired, achy, and don't want to do anything. Try taking some time off from school or work to spend this week with your child. Decrease the number of screens your child uses (TV, tablets, laptops, and phones) and give your child as much of your time as they need so as not to increase the child's stress levels.

During the pandemic, you don't need to worry about your child too much. If possible, keep them away from public places, so that they are not exposed to people with coughs. It is important for you not to leave your child alone in case you must go out.

Many people have been complaining that they haven't had a chance to get to know each other. Well, you don't have to worry about your child not having friends or being sad that they don't get lots of time from you.

After all, there are a lot of people going through the same things as we do. It will take some time to think about what we can do for each other and how we can make this world a better one.

Tips to keep calm at home:

1. Decide what you will do if the pandemic lasts for a long time.
2. Put some chocolate in your child's school bag so that they won't get bored. Store some food in your fridge for them as well.
3. Keep your child busy at home, help them choose a hobby, and use their imagination to make their day better or safer.
4. Bring up the money-related issues: how to prepare for different scenarios and how to manage them, which financial documents should be brought along with you, and which clothes you should pack first.
5. Since your child will be stressed, try to make them smile by playing a favorite game with them.

# Conclusion

Children are the most wonderful gifts in our lives. The world is a better place because there are little ones like these running about and getting up to mischief. Even though parenting is difficult and dealing with this renegade creature is intimidating, the unconditional love and tie that exists between these two people is what holds this lovely relationship together like a blossoming flower. Children are not born explosive. They have their own experiences as they interact with the rest of civilization. However, their parents and the environment in which they are raised have a significant effect on their growth, both intellectually and physically. Every explosive youngster is a result of something that caused him or her to become explosive in the first place.

There is nothing impossible in this world and coping with your explosive child is the same. Unquestionably, you can deal with your infant in a variety of methods that are addressed in this book, and I am certain that you will agree with what has been shared here. You will be able to see trends, search for answers, observe changes in results, and create a more positive environment for your child if you follow these steps. Children are nothing more than sponges, soaking up whatever we put in front of them. If we continue to dump our frustrations and anger on them for the way they express their feelings, we will eventually end up building small explosives out of their emotions.

Now that you know the secret to dealing with your special one, you can go ahead and indicate anything you believe will be the most beneficial for you and your child to endure this difficult period in your life together. Though this small one will grow up to be an adult with a dazzling personality and special skills, you will always remember those days when they made you want to give up on yourself. Because these are the days when you will feel the most connected to them and engage with them. So, make the most of this time!

# Author's Note

Dear reader,

I hope you enjoyed my book.

Please don't forget to toss up a quick review on amazon, I will personally read it! Positive or negative, I'm grateful for all feedback.

Reviews are so helpful for self-published authors and your feedback can make such a difference for my book!

Thanks very much for your time, and I look forward to hearing from you soon.

Sincerely,

Rachel